TODAY
IN MY GARDEN

D0862021

Foreword by TOBY BOST

COOL SPRINGS PRESS
FRANKLIN, TENNESSEE

Published by Cool Springs Press, 101 Forrest Crossing Boulevard,
Franklin, Tennessee 37064

Dunn, Teri. Today in my garden : 365 tips for your Southern garden /
Teri Dunn; foreword by Toby Bost.
p. cm.
ISBN-10: 1-59186-342-2 (pbk.)
ISBN-13: 978-1-59186-342-7
1. Gardening—Southern States. I. Title. II.
Title: 365 tips for your Southern garden.
SB451.34.S68D86 2006
635.0975—dc22
2006027989

First Printing: 2006
Printed in Canada
10 9 8 7 6 5 4 3 2 1

Visit the Cool Springs Press website at **www.coolspringspress.net**.

DEDICATION

To the volunteers of botanical
gardens and arboreta across the South
who give their time so generously.
These unsung heroes drive hundreds of
miles, eat brown-bag lunches, greet
garden guests with wide smiles, and
share their plant knowledge graciously.
They deserve a round of applause;
thank you all for caring!
—*Toby*

CONTENTS

FOREWORD

APPENDIX

❦ EVERYDAY TIP ❦

Get into the habit of keeping a garden journal. It's like a "baby album" for your garden. It is invaluable for jotting down notes about problems or successes, storing articles from newspapers or magazines, or attaching photos. It doesn't have to be fancy, but spiral binding, tabbed pages, and pockets are convenient. (It makes a great gift, too!)

FOREWORD

Welcome! *Today in My Garden* is a marvelous way to gain the wisdom of experts and simplify gardening using timely reminders. Gardening tips can be like rays of sunshine that fall your way when the chips are down. A little wisdom, at the right time, may be all the encouragement you need to give it a go for another season, espe-cially if you've had a rough gardening year. A novice can jumpstart their gardening experience with this handy little book. And for more experienced gardeners, starting your day with a handy gardening tip will fuel your curiosity to learn more. And while gardening is a hobby, it is in every sense a science as well. From caring for indoor plants to planting your first rose garden, it often takes more than just a green thumb. (I'll let you in on a secret: The proverbial "green thumb" has much to do with knowing *what* to do and *when*.)

GARDEN DIVERSITY

Gardening in the South can be a year-round proposition, and for newcomers that can be a blessing or a curse. For gardeners from colder climes, this is good news! Four seasons are common in the upper South with our azaleas, flowering cherries, and tall fescue lawns. While in the lower South—though winter color can be rather drab when the Bermudagrass lawn goes dormant—lucky gardeners can enjoy a longer season with perennial flowers, camellias, and tropicals.

Along with the plant diversity found in the South comes a greater need for maintenance advice, considering the vast array of both herbaceous and woody ornamentals we grow. And of course, again the questions—what must I do *today*? When is the best season to prune this or fertilize that? Attentive gardeners are rewarded for keeping a keen eye on the progress of their gardens. (We call it "scouting" in agricultural circles, or monitoring the development of fungus diseases and marauding insects that are all too common to southerners.) Our humid weather and high rainfall are justifiable causes for alarm in the South.

Part of the intrigue I had with gardening as a child was observing plant diversity, especially flowers in a neighbor's garden. Later, my decision to change direction from a college education major to horticulture as a career had much to do with my fascination for greenhouse plants. The mystery of gardening often manifests itself as unanswered questions. Now after many years of hands-on puttering around in my garden and networking with other gardeners, a vast amount of information is at my disposal. With the advent of computers, gardeners can get lots of information and can organize a database or folder for tracking good tips. Yet, I still value the wisdom of true gardeners as they share their daily tips in a book such as this one.

Today in My Garden

The older I get, the more I depend on my "to do" lists. Normally the list comes out each morning after I drink my cup of coffee and take a little time to stretch and meditate. Successful gardeners make lists and some may even journal or photograph their gardens from time to time. My advice to the garden newbie is to make note of all the advice you get from seasoned gardeners. The "over-the-fence" wisdom from a Master Gardener or Extension agent is worth a formal course in landscape gardening.

Through the years I have kept a personal gardening journal that is replete with sage advice from veterans, freely

given and welcomed, in my early years
as a landscape professional. Of course,
some of the old plant favorites from
years ago have been replaced by superior
hybrids and disease-resistant cultivars.

Those of us who enjoy gardening
often prefer to do the work ourselves.
The labor, though strenuous at times,
is so rewarding, especially when the
rose beds have been pruned or the lawn
mowed before the next rain storm blows
in. We are caretakers of God's earth and

our gardens give back to us. Renewed vigor and mental well-being are often overlooked benefits of gardening but if you consider the camaraderie with fellow gardeners, can life get any better? So, welcome friends, to *Today in My Garden*.

—*Toby Bost*

❖ SPRING ❖

❖ Everyday Tip ❖

If you haven't already
done so, sketch a map of your
garden (it can be simple!)
noting the areas that receive full
sun, a mix of sun and shade,
or full shade. Knowing this is
invaluable to selecting the right
plant, for the right spot.

❧ TIP 1 ❧

Fill a windowbox with early spring
flowers. First make sure any
remnants of last year's show have
been scraped out. Put in fresh
potting soil. Arrange the plants atop
the soil first, and shift them around
if you wish—sort of a dress
rehearsal. Then plant them
at the level they were in the pot, and
water everything thoroughly.

❏ *Check when completed*

✤ TIP 2 ✤

Check out the garden soil. It may still be too soon to plant much, but it doesn't hurt to get acquainted. Scoop up a handful and squeeze. If the dirt oozes moisture, it's too soon. If it forms a ball that breaks apart when poked by your finger, it's okay to sow early and cold-tolerant crops (like lettuces, cabbages, and radishes).

❏ *Check when completed*

❧ TIP 3 ❧

Got dandelions? Don't let them go to seed! Even if you lack the time and energy to dig up each plant by the roots (remember, these have very long taproots), at least remove the furry yellow flowers before they become white balls of drifting seeds. A pass of the lawnmower should do the trick.

❑ *Check when completed*

❦ TIP 4 ❦

Don't forget our feathered
friends! Take some
time to check bird feeders and
houses. Clean out and
repair houses before nesting
season. Clean bird
feeders of old, moldy seed and
fill with fresh food.

❑ *Check when completed*

MARCH

❧ TIP 5 ❧

The first time to feed your
roses is after they have already leafed
out and flower buds are beginning
to swell and show a bit of color.
Special fertilizers are sold for roses,
but you can also use an all-purpose,
slow-release formula. Deliver
the food with plenty of water
so it all soaks in.

❏ *Check when completed*

❖ TIP 6 ❖

When watering shrubs, rosebushes, and trees, a slow, deep soaking is much better than occasional lighter sprinklings. Set the hose at the base of the plant, at a slow trickle, and come back in an hour or so. Check with a trowel to see whether moisture has penetrated. If not, water for another hour or until you are satisfied.

❏ *Check when completed*

❖ TIP 7 ❖

Don't rush when planting
corn—the seeds languish or even rot
in cold, damp ground. Wait until
the soil has warmed up. Plant an
inch or two deep; shallower
plantings tend to sprout faster
because they are nearer to the
ground surface, which is warmer.
Always sow more than you think
you'll need; you can thin later.

❑ *Check when completed*

❧ TIP 8 ❧

This is a good time to prune
any frost-damaged plants
back to live wood. Proper
cuts will heal without incident.
Then, fertilize with slow-
release plant food.

❏ *Check when completed*

❧ TIP 9 ❧

Keep a close eye on your
fruit trees. As soon as the buds
begin to swell, you may spray them
with dormant oil. To be effective,
the temperature must be over 45
degrees Fahrenheit. This mainly
helps to control scale, but it thwarts
other pests, as well.

☐ *Check when completed*

❖ TIP 10 ❖

Rake the lawn. This gets
out any debris, trash, straggling
leaves, and weeds from last year. It
also helps the grass stand up after
months of being matted down, and
lets in air and light. All this is
conducive to getting your lawn off
to a good growing season.

❑ *Check when completed*

❧ TIP 11 ❧

A big pot need not be
super-heavy. Don't fill it completely
with potting soil when the plants
within use only a few inches' worth.
Instead, put a layer of foam peanuts
in the bottom first. Nobody will
know, the plants will be fine, and
you'll be able to pick up the pot
and move it if you want.

❑ *Check when completed*

❧ TIP 12 ❧

Weed with a sharp hoe. It will be
a quicker and easier way to
dispatch a crowd of young weeds.
Keep your strokes shallow,
though—you don't want to harm
the roots of the desirable plants
or bring more weed seeds
to the surface.

❏ *Check when completed*

❧ TIP 13 ❧

Leave fading bulb foliage alone
so it can send nutrients to fuel next
year's show down into the bulb
below. The leaves will yellow and
flag, and no, the process isn't
pretty. Bending over handfuls and
cinching them with a rubber band
has no benefits, though it may
look slightly better.

❏ *Check when completed*

✤ TIP 14 ✤

If you are growing fruit trees,
establish a regular fungicide
spray schedule to begin with bud-
break. Your local Extension
Service office can recommend the
best fruit tree varieties for
your area, if you'd like to
investigate further.

❑ *Check when completed*

❧ TIP 15 ❧

Now or later in summer is a fine
time to remove a tree limb.
Assuming it's not too thick or too
high up, you can do this yourself
with a good sharp handsaw. Use the
three-cuts method: an undercut
halfway up; an overcut a bit farther
out and halfway down (at this point,
the branch snaps right off); then a
neat cut at the branch collar.

☐ *Check when completed*

❖ TIP 16 ❖

Divide overgrown perennials,
ones in large clumps, or ones that
seem to be less productive every
year. Discard the center of the old
plant and save the outer sections—
make sure each piece has a good
clump of roots and some emerging
green growth. Replant, evenly
spaced, and water well.

❏ *Check when completed*

❧ TIP 17 ❧

Celebrate St. Patrick's Day
with your own green carnations!
Just buy some white ones, recut
their bases, and put them in a vase
of water to which you have added
several drops of green food coloring.
After a few hours, if the color is too
light, take out the flowers for a
moment and stir in a few more
drops of food coloring.

❑ *Check when completed*

❧ TIP 18 ❧

Thinking of moving a shrub or
small tree to a new location?
Spring is a great time to do this,
while the plant is still dormant (so it
won't be traumatized). So when it
does start growing, it can direct all
its energy into a great show. Just be
sure the soil is workable before
undertaking this project.

❏ *Check when completed*

❧ TIP 19 ❧

Now that the soil is warmer
and the air temperatures are milder,
you can plant container-grown trees
and shrubs. You want to get them
into the ground now so spring rains
can water them in for you and, of
course, to get them going before
summer heat arrives.

☐ *Check when completed*

❖ TIP 20 ❖

When there is no more danger of
frost, you can move your potted
houseplants outside. But ease them
into outdoor life. Even if they
are sun-lovers, put them in a
sheltered and shady location, so they
can adjust. Gradually move
them to a brighter location over a
period of days or weeks.

❑ *Check when completed*

❖ TIP 21 ❖

Decorate a lamppost! Wrap it
with a 4-foot-tall, slender piece of
chicken wire, overlapping the ends
and cinching them tightly in place
(use wire cutters rather than your
fingers—it's easier on your hands).
Then plant a climbing vine right at
the base. By midsummer, foliage
and flowers will hide the wire and
the post will be a pretty sight.

❏ *Check when completed*

❖ TIP 22 ❖

It's finally okay to fertilize
growing plants, including those that
you pruned a few weeks ago.
Water before and after feeding. Use
an all-purpose garden fertilizer for
most all your plants, and purchase
special fertilizers for plants with
special needs. Whatever you use,
always apply according to the
label instructions.

❏ *Check when completed*

❖ TIP 23 ❖

Buy some ear plugs. Garden equipment that you will soon be using—whether lawn mower, rototiller, or chainsaw—is noisy. Indeed, some machines can hit 100 decibels, which is harmful if we subject ourselves to the din repeatedly. Wearing protection is also a nice way to signal that you want to be left alone to concentrate on your work!

❏ *Check when completed*

❧ TIP 24 ❧

If rainfall is sparse this year, you must be a diligent waterer (but do not overwater); about 1 inch per week. This is especially important for any young vegetable, herb, and flower seedlings. If these little plants dry out too much when they are just starting out, they grow poorly and may never prosper.

❏ *Check when completed*

❧ TIP 25 ❧

Now is the time to start removing
any winter mulch—compost, pine
straw, some other organic material,
whatever you laid down last fall—
from your flowerbeds. Wait until the
temperatures are above freezing.
Remove it gradually. Use your
hands, a rake, a leaf blower, or even
some strong blasts from the hose.

❏ *Check when completed*

❧ TIP 26 ❧

Keep cats from treating your flowerbeds like a litter box. Lay down some chicken wire and cover it lightly with soil or mulch—they don't like the way their paws get snagged. Alternatively, try sprinkling an unpleasant-smelling repellent around: hot pepper, black pepper, citronella oil, even coffee grounds.

❏ *Check when completed*

❧ TIP 27 ❧

Zap weeds in the cracks of your sidewalk, walkway, patio, or driveway, one by one, safely. Just fill a spray bottle with white vinegar (with a few drops of dish soap to contribute stickiness) and hit each one with a strong blast. If the weed isn't dead in a day, spray it again—it should succumb.

❑ *Check when completed*

❧ TIP 28 ❧

Remove diseased, infested, or dead leaves whenever you see them. Don't let them just fall off and hang around the base of your plants, where they can harbor and encourage problems. Get that stuff out—way out. Don't even toss it on your compost pile. Send it away with the household garbage.

❑ *Check when completed*

❖ TIP 29 ❖

Pull weeds out by the roots. They compete with your plants, especially the new and smaller ones, hogging valuable resources of soil nutrients, water, and sunlight. Often they harbor insects and plant diseases, too. Note that it is much easier to get out the entire weed when the ground is damp, after a rain or shortly after you've watered.

❑ *Check when completed*

❖ TIP 30 ❖

Make patch repairs to your lawn.
Rake the bare spots beforehand, and
then broadcast grass seed as evenly
as you can. Scatter or broadcast
seed-starter fertilizer, then top off
with a thin layer of soil. Water
gently with a sprinkler today, and
daily until the grass has sprouted
and is growing well.

❑ *Check when completed*

❖ TIP 31 ❖

This is a good time to sow warm-season grasses. Clear out the planting area, add weed-free organic matter, and rake smooth. If you don't use a mechanical seeder, just broadcast left to right, and then up and down, to make sure the whole area is covered. Keep moist so the seeds can germinate.

❑ *Check when completed*

❧ TIP 32 ❧

Combat pesky rabbits. Garden
centers sell special "rabbit fencing,"
which is a bigger mesh than chicken
wire. Wrap individual plants or
envelop a flowerbed or the vegetable
patch. Be sure to sink the fencing
down into the ground by several
inches, so they cannot get under.

❑ *Check when completed*

❧ TIP 33 ❧

If a deer fence is not practical for your yard, you may have some luck discouraging deer with repellents. You'll find plenty of products sold for this purpose, though they ought to be replenished after a rain. Or suspend—on string or twine— bars of soap from branches. (Irish Spring and Lifebuoy are particularly intense.)

❑ *Check when completed*

❧ TIP 34 ❧

Mulch around the bases of your perennials, or renew depleted mulch. A good mulch layer helps keep burgeoning weed populations at bay and helps retain soil moisture. Be careful, however, not to push the mulch flush up against the stems or crown of the plant, which can invite rot. Leave about an inch of space.

❑ *Check when completed*

❧ TIP 35 ❧

Check on established vines
as well as ones you planted this year.
Most are surging into growth.
If you don't intervene sooner rather
than later, and direct the stems where
you want them to go, the whole
display can get out of control pretty
quickly. Train and tie elongating
branches onto supports with strips
of old nylons or soft cloth.

❑ *Check when completed*

❧ TIP 36 ❧

Tall-growing perennials often benefit from staking—foxgloves, hollyhocks, verbascums, penstemons, and dahlias, to name a few. If you didn't insert something at planting time, it's probably not too late. Just poke the support securely into the ground close by, and attach the plant to it at intervals with soft ties.

❏ *Check when completed*

❧ Tip 37 ❧

Nip insect-pest problems early. When you see harmful bugs or beetles dining on your flowerbeds or in your vegetable garden, handpick and toss them in a bucket of soapy water. If you don't know their identity, look them up in a gardening book or show a sample to someone knowledgeable such as an Extension agent so you can fight off infestations.

❏ *Check when completed*

❧ TIP 38 ❧

Bermudagrass and other warm-season grasses may now start growing, so you can begin watering the lawn regularly and fertilize occasionally. Remember that lawn fertilizer is most effective on recently watered grass. But don't overdo either the watering or the fertilizer—let the lawn grow at a steady pace.

❑ *Check when completed*

❧ TIP 39 ❧

Once flowers have faded, dig up
traditional spring-flowering bulbs
such as daffodils, hyacinths, and
crocus. Instead of discarding them,
wipe the dirt off and store them in
labeled bags in a dark, cool place.
You can chill and replant them
later—for now, it's fine for them
to rest in dormancy.

❑ *Check when completed*

❧ TIP 40 ❧

Are you growing fruit trees, like a plum or peach? Have you noticed the crops for some years are big, and other years are disappointing? Early spring is the perfect time to intervene to make things more even and predictable. If this is a good year, thin the fruits. Pick off and dispose of half the fruit while it is still tiny.

❏ *Check when completed*

❖ TIP 41 ❖

Be on the lookout for aphids, and act quickly if you see them. These tiny sucking insects relish the new growth on roses, fruit trees, and shrubs, but they also go after your flowerbeds and vegetable garden. Blast them with the hose or an insecticidal soap; make sure you get the bottoms of the leaves, too.

❏ *Check when completed*

❧ TIP 42 ❧

Spread compost. Whether store-bought or homemade, it is always beneficial for your garden, especially early in the season. Because compost is sometimes still decomposing, it generates some heat, a hedge against springtime's temperature swings. Sprinkle to a depth of 1 to 3 inches, broadcasting it by hand, or with a trowel or shovel.

❑ *Check when completed*

❖ TIP 43 ❖

Plant annuals. This is a fine
time to put out marigolds, cleome,
and cosmos. Be sure to water in
each one well and to water
consistently over the coming days
and weeks so they can "get their legs
under them" and prosper. Top off
the planting area with some
moisture-retaining mulch.

❑ *Check when completed*

❧ TIP 44 ❧

Always wear gloves when working in the garden. Stinging caterpillars, poison ivy, and yellow jackets are potential dangers. You can keep several pairs of inexpensive ones around to "save" your good ones.

❏ *Check when completed*

APRIL

· TIP 45 ·

Pick bouquets often! It's one
of the great rewards of gardening,
plus the very process of going out
and selecting flowers compels
you to examine—and enjoy—your
plants as you go by. Bring a water
bucket and plunk in the stems as
you go. This keeps everything fresh
until you get inside, where you can
groom and shorten each stem.

❏ *Check when completed*

❧ TIP 46 ❧

If you haven't already done so, go ahead and direct-sow seeds of favorite vegetables directly into prepared garden soil. Melons of various kinds, including watermelon, can go in now, as can squash and cucumbers. Cover them over after planting, and be diligent about watering regularly so they can germinate.

❑ *Check when completed*

❧ TIP 47 ❧

Plant herbs in the ground,
in pots, or in windowboxes.
Wherever you grow them, make
sure they have suitable soil. It does
not have to be especially dark and
rich (which can lead to overly lush
or lanky growth), but it should be
well drained to prevent root rot.

☐ *Check when completed*

❖ TIP 48 ❖

As the weather grows gradually hotter, mulch can be either a blessing or a curse. Check all your mulched plants to see how they are faring. Up to three inches is good for most; replenish as necessary. If you use more than that, any necessary water may not be able to get through to the root systems.

❑ *Check when completed*

❧ TIP 49 ❧

Now is a fine time to lay sod,
especially suitable for slopes. Prepare
the area by stripping away former
plantings and removing rocks,
weeds, and roots. Till lightly to
loosen the soil, sprinkle a little lawn
fertilizer (follow the amount
directions on the bag), and rake
smooth. Put the sod down on a
cool, cloudy day, and water well.

❏ *Check when completed*

❧ TIP 50 ❧

Plan to sketch or photograph your flowerbeds when they are at their peaks. Not only will the images be a source of pride, but they'll also provide useful information when you view them with care later. You'll be able to identify successful combinations, as well as ones that didn't work out—all fodder for deciding on next year's plans.

❏ *Check when completed*

❧ TIP 51 ❧

Fertilize your container-grown
plants every week now, particularly
those that flower or that you
hope will flower. Use an all-purpose
plant food and dilute it according to
label directions. Foliar feeding
is an alternative option whereby you
spray the dilute solution right on
the leaves. Either way, deliver
the food with water.

❑ *Check when completed*

❧ TIP 52 ❧

Allow wildflowers to go to
seed and try collecting the seed
yourself for later replanting. Pick
the stalks and hang them upside
down in a warm, dark place. If the
flower heads are the sort that
"shatters," simply bag the tops in
order to capture falling seeds.

❏ *Check when completed*

❧ TIP 53 ❧

Feed Bermuda and zoysia lawns
after spring green-up. The type of
fertilizer, and amount, depends on
the type of grass you are growing,
so be sure you know. When in
doubt, get advice from garden-
center staff or a landscaper. Then, if
you can't count on April showers,
water well so it can soak in.

❑ *Check when completed*

❧ TIP 54 ❧

Get in the habit of forming a basin
around every plant you install or
move. It should be around the
perimeter of the plant's topgrowth
"drip line" (the outer edge). Mound
soil up a few inches in a circle
around the plant. Then, when you
water, it will go straight to the roots.
A basin also holds mulch well.

❏ *Check when completed*

❧ TIP 55 ❧

Dried flowers for arrangements
and craft projects are easy
to make. Just remember that
whatever form or stage the blooms
are in, that's how they'll dry, with no
changes. Array them on screens in a
hot, dry, well-ventilated room. Or
place them in plastic boxes of
silica gel for a few days.

☐ *Check when completed*

❧ TIP 56 ❧

Make a mini water garden in a tub or kettle. It must be 18 inches deep to host a potted water lily (ask the nursery about ones that do well in smaller quarters). Or try other attractive aquatics, both floaters and tall ones like irises, papyrus, and taro. Full sun is best. Top off the water when it evaporates a bit.

❑ *Check when completed*

❧ TIP 57 ❧

Time to remind your forsythia bush who's boss! Once all the flowers have faded, the branches will elongate like crazy until the plant is way out of bounds. While this is not a plant for a clipped and formal look, it will look better (and grow more densely) with a late spring haircut. Use sharp clippers or a hedge trimmer.

❑ *Check when completed*

❧ TIP 58 ❧

Deadhead both annuals and
perennials. That is, pinch or cut off
spent flowers promptly. Otherwise,
the plants may be tempted to
spend a lot of energy going to seed
and the flower show will end. This
way, you persuade them to redirect
their energy into making a fresh
round of flowers.

❏ *Check when completed*

❧ TIP 59 ❧

It's okay to set out tomato seedlings, in the ground or in large tubs or pots. If cooler weather threatens, just be prepared to drape plastic over them overnight or use a Wall-o-Water™. Set plants a little deeper than they were in the pot or flat— new roots will develop from the stems and help anchor them.

❑ *Check when completed*

❧ TIP 60 ❧

It's easy to repair a broken clay pot. Here's what to do: Glue it back together with carpenter's glue (not white glue, which is water-soluble). Wrap the pot with masking tape to hold everything together while the glue dries. Give it a few days, then remove the tape, add potting mix and plants, and you're back in business.

❏ *Check when completed*

❦ TIP 61 ❦

Continue planting warm-
season vegetables in an area that is
well prepared with moisture-
retaining organic matter. Raised
beds are ideal. Vegetables that
prosper now include corn, melons,
okra, sweet and hot peppers,
squash, and tomatoes.

❏ *Check when completed*

❧ TIP 62 ❧

Plant heat-loving annuals.
There should be plenty for sale at
local outlets—petunias, lantana, and
salvia are favorites. Larger plants,
while a bit more expensive, have a
better chance of doing well this
time of year. In any event, water
them upon planting and often
in the coming weeks (even twice
weekly if it's very hot).

❑ *Check when completed*

❧ TIP 63 ❧

If you want to get serious about
controlling grubs in your lawn, now
is the time, when they are close to
the surface. The most common
control is "milky spore disease,"
which is organic and effective. For
application rates, consult the label.
(By the way, just so you know,
grubs grow up to be either June
bugs or Japanese beetles.)

❑ *Check when completed*

❧ TIP 64 ❧

Lawn grass may be growing
lustily now, especially if there has
been rain. Don't let grass get
too high, or it will be hard to mow.
Make a habit out of cutting it at
least weekly, and don't forget you
can leave the clippings to break
down naturally.

❑ *Check when completed*

❖ TIP 65 ❖

Thin those flowers that are
susceptible to mildew—before
mildew has a chance to get started
and mar your display. Summer
phlox, asters, and bee balm are all
vulnerable. So take a few plants out
of the stand, here and there. If you
dig them up, replant them elsewhere
in the yard or give them away.

❑ *Check when completed*

❧ TIP 66 ❧

Weed-whacking is not a fun chore, but these tips will make the project faster and more efficient. If possible, work in the late afternoon, past the heat of the day, when the plants are drier. Make sure the tool is clean and you have fresh "string" reeled out several inches. Wear socks, long pants, and eye protection.

❏ *Check when completed*

❧ TIP 67 ❧

Manage your mint. This tasty herb, unfortunately, starts to grow rampantly as the soil warms up. So act early. Dig up and discard sprouts growing where you don't want them. Confine the rest in a bottomless plastic container (such as a gallon milk jug), pushed down into the ground around the clump.

❑ *Check when completed*

❧ Tip 68 ❧

Remember your hanging
baskets! In warmer weather, they
dry out amazingly quickly. Use a
watering wand and soak thoroughly
in the mornings. A "mulch" of
damp moss, an inch or so thick,
arrayed over the soil surface helps
retain moisture between waterings.
Just scoot it aside when watering
and reposition it after.

❏ *Check when completed*

❖ TIP 69 ❖

Are the lower leaves of your tomato
plants turning yellow? Plant diseases
that develop in hot weather when
air circulation is poor cause this. If
the plant is not too bushy yet,
installing a tomato cage may impove
air circulation. Also be sure to water
right at ground level; never let water
splash up onto the leaves.

❑ *Check when completed*

❧ Tip 70 ❧

Combat leaf-roll caterpillars
on your cannas. If you don't
intervene, they will literally
perforate the leaves. You can spray
the worms to beat them back.
Alternatively, cut the stalks back to
the ground and wait for new ones to
be generated—it won't take long.

❑ *Check when completed*

❧ TIP 71 ❧

Install a new brick or flagstone path—a much easier job in drier weather. Carve out the course with a shovel to a depth of several inches, then fill with a base of sand or sand dust. Wiggle the bricks or stones into place, separating them by an inch or less. Water down, let settle, and add more sand if needed.

❑ *Check when completed*

❧ TIP 72 ❧

Be vigilant about spider mites
on your evergreens. These voracious
little pests can suck the life out of
your plants, leaving yellowing
needles and webs in their wake. Hit
the plants with strong jets of water
from the hose to dislodge them;
then repeat weekly as needed.

☐ *Check when completed*

❧ TIP 73 ❦

Give rampant-growing hedges
another haircut! Use freshly
sharpened clippers and loppers. If
the plants are thorny or twiggy, wear
a long-sleeved shirt and tough
gloves as you work. Remove suckers
emerging from the bases. Clip back
new growth all around to inspire
a thicker profile.

❑ *Check when completed*

❖ TIP 74 ❖

Have your marigolds turned
to lace? If so, suspect slugs. Go on a
night safari to see what's eating
them. If it is slugs, try the beer trick.
Place a shallow dish filled with stale
beer by the plants; by morning, any
slugs attracted to the beer will be
drowned or too drunk to care.

❏ *Check when completed*

❦ TIP 75 ❦

Take a close look at your
azaleas. If you spot hard green,
brown, or white growths or
thickened leaves, these are fungal
galls—and you ought to remove
them. They occur most often
in wet years. Just pick them off
and dispose of them.

☐ *Check when completed*

❧ TIP 76 ❧

Check on your compost pile.
Hot weather causes the contents to
break down faster, and you
may find you have a bounty of
"black gold." If you don't use
it, it will continue to break down.
Instead, scoop it out and
use it around the yard as a
nourishing mulch.

❏ *Check when completed*

❖ TIP 77 ❖

Check the pots of houseplants that
you've moved outside for the
summer. Remember that the smaller
their containers are, the faster the
plants will dry out. If you can't
always think to check them, then
plunking in a color-coded
moisture meter to alert you may
be a good solution.

❏ *Check when completed*

❧ TIP 78 ❧

Tender foliage plants may now go
in the ground—caladiums and
elephant ear, especially. Small starter
plants should be for sale down at the
garden center, but these plants
will grow well from bare tubers, too.
Be sure to supply the organically
rich, moist soil they relish.

☐ *Check when completed*

❖ TIP 79 ❖

Cut back young mum plants now. Though it seems brutal, this operation causes them to grow shorter but bushier (left alone, they can get leggy and fall over). They will bloom better as a result, and the plants will stronger.

❑ *Check when completed*

❧ Tip 80 ❧

If you weren't happy with the
location or numbers of some of your
spring bulbs, it is safe to dig them
up and move them elsewhere in the
yard. Their foliage should have died
down by now, or nearly so, and thus
they should be practically
dormant—an optimum time to
make your move.

❏ *Check when completed*

❧ TIP 81 ❧

If you are growing leafy
herbs for harvest, prevent them
from going to seed by pinching off
flowers when they develop. This
forces the plants to continue
producing tasty leaves and prevents
self-sowing. Last but not least, it
thwarts bees, which are more
interested in the flowers than any
other part of the plant, of course.

❑ *Check when completed*

❖ TIP 82 ❖

When the weather starts to get hotter, watering often, and enough, can become a real chore. Get some soaker hoses and thread them through the flowerbeds, ground-cover area, vegetable garden, or any other spot that needs regular moisture. For these, as well as for sprinklers, consider investing in a timer that installs at the faucet.

❑ *Check when completed*

⚜ TIP 83 ⚜

Sweet-potato cuttings (called "slips") are for sale now. Because these mature into truly impressive vines, prepare an ample area where they can grow freely—a foot between each plant is good, and four-foot-wide rows work well. Water well at planting time, and provide some shade for a few days or a week until they get going.

❏ *Check when completed*

❧ TIP 84 ❧

Some plants develop powdery mildew as summer comes on, thanks to the heat and humidity. In particular, the leaves of lilacs, roses, phlox, and green beans turn powdery white. There's not much you can do, except try to improve air circulation within and around the plants with a little judicious clipping. In the future, plant resistant varieties.

❑ *Check when completed*

❧ TIP 85 ❧

The weed wars are far from over.
Under no circumstances should you
let annual weeds go to seed! This is
how they create a population
explosion. Perennial weeds will
spread if you don't stop them.
Thwart all of them by chopping off
their heads, yanking them out, or
both. For tough weeds, paint cut
stems with a weed killer.

❏ *Check when completed*

❧ TIP 86 ❧

Walk through and double-check all your plant supports, from tomato cages to staked hollyhocks. Rampant growth and full weight may have caused them to lean or pulled them down. Reinsert stakes securely into the ground, replace missing ties, and add more ties as needed. In other words, reestablish order.

❑ *Check when completed*

❖ TIP 87 ❖

Float rose petals in a punch
or sangria, or scatter them over
buttercream-frosted cake or cup-
cakes. Pick them on a hot afternoon
when the fragrance is at its peak;
rinse them gently (especially important if you have sprayed your
rosebushes), pat dry, then store in a
plastic bag in the refrigerator for a
few hours before using.

❏ *Check when completed*

❧ TIP 88 ❧

Keep pots of herbs near the kitchen for spontaneous summer meals. Ones that do well in a container include rosemary, cilantro, sage, parsley, oregano, chives, and thyme. Water in the morning and cut the same evening you use them for maximum flavor; cut only as much as you need. Rinse off any dust or dirt before using.

❏ *Check when completed*

❖ TIP 89 ❖

Soil testing—*before* planting
a new lawn or garden—is an
important step. It's not difficult to
perform and is generally
inexpensive. Check with your
Extension Service for test
kits and instructions.

❑ *Check when completed*

❧ TIP 90 ❧

Plant some annuals now that both
air and soil are warm enough. But
avoid the temptation to buy blooming plants—the transition from
their pampered life at the garden
center to your yard may cause them
to drop their petals. They'll recover,
of course, but it's smarter to buy
annuals with plenty of good buds.

❑ *Check when completed*

❖ SUMMER ❖

❦ EVERYDAY TIP ❦

Enjoy your garden.
In the midst of chores and to-do
lists, you might overlook
why it's such a pleasure. Sit outside,
read a book, take a stroll,
snooze in a hammock, have a
party—reap the rewards.

❧ TIP 91 ❧

As the weather gets hotter,
lawn growth of some lawn grasses
will slow down. This is your
cue to stop fertilizing and water
every few weeks (assuming
there is no rain). You should also
mow less often—and raise the
mower height. All these things
help the grass cope.

❑ *Check when completed*

❧ TIP 92 ❧

Visit the shrubs, rosebushes, and trees that you planted this spring and give each one a tune-up. (You should already be supplying good soaking waterings.) Check for signs of disease and insect pests. Cut off all afflicted plant parts and get rid of them. (But save a small amount if you need a diagnosis and advice on treatment.)

❏ *Check when completed*

❖ TIP 93 ❖

Black sooty mold may appear on the leaves of some plants. Sticky honeydew is attracting it. And that is being generated by thrips, aphids, whiteflies, or spider mites. If the problem is extensive, your best bet is to spray with an insecticidal soap. Be sure to spray the undersides of the leaves, as well.

☐ *Check when completed*

❖ TIP 94 ❖

Deadhead your annuals.
That is, pinch or cut off spent
flowers promptly. Otherwise, the
plants may be tempted to spend a
lot of energy going to seed and the
flower show will end. This way, you
might persuade them to redirect
their energy into making a fresh
round of flowers.

☐ *Check when completed*

❧ TIP 95 ❧

Help the plants in your
vegetable garden cope with the
heat. Lay down or replenish the
mulch layer at their feet—up to
3 inches thick is not excessive.
Compost is perfect, but pine
straw and bark mulch will serve
as well. (If you don't do this,
blossom-end rot can occur.)

❑ *Check when completed*

⸙ TIP 96 ⸙

If your area experiences a long hot or dry spell, refrain from fertilizing. Fertilizer is most effective when plants are well hydrated and their soil is damp; otherwise, the food never reaches the roots or can "burn" them. Freshly fed plants tend to put on a flush of new growth, which would be instantly stressed by the blazing weather.

❑ *Check when completed*

❖ TIP 97 ❖

Look before you squish a garden
bug! Not all are harmful pests.
When in doubt as to a critter's
identity, look him up in gardening
books or take one (in a jar) to a
garden center staffer. If it is a pest,
you can get advice on how to
combat it and buy any product you
might need while there. (Ask for
biological controls, first.)

☐ *Check when completed*

❧ TIP 98 ❧

Pick ripe squash, okra, cucumbers,
and eggplants. When you keep
up the harvest, the plants are
inspired to keep on producing.
Go out in the early morning—less
heat stress for you, plus the plants
are full of moisture then and the
produce will be tastier.

❏ *Check when completed*

❧ TIP 99 ❧

Last call for pruning and
shaping your spring-flowering
shrubs! As their flowers begin
to fade, the plant will start
devoting energy to producing new
flower buds. If that process starts
before you come along with your
clippers, you will reduce next year's
show—a real shame.

☐ *Check when completed*

❧ TIP 100 ❧

Berry plants will soon start to
ripen their sweet harvest. But there's
competition for the fruit—birds,
wild animals perhaps, and various
insect pests. Luckily, they can all be
thwarted the same way, if you act
early. Drape the plants in netting;
garden-supply shops and mail-order
suppliers sell large-enough pieces
with the right mesh.

❏ *Check when completed*

✣ TIP 101 ✣

Your tomatoes are just
starting to form fruits now. But in
order to ensure a tasty harvest, you
must keep the plants evenly
watered. Of course, you might just
pick a few green ones and make
some fried green tomatoes—always
a tasty summertime treat!

❑ *Check when completed*

❧ TIP 102 ❧

Algae problem in your birdbath?
Assuming you've cleaned it (a
mixture of equal parts of vinegar
and water works well and is
nontoxic for the birds), there's one
other thing you can try. Pick about
six stems off your lavender plant,
wrap them with a rubber band, and
float the bundle in the water.

☐ *Check when completed*

❧ TIP 103 ❧

Set out a hummingbird feeder!
Red-dyed sugar water is now con-
sidered unneeded and possibly not
good for the little birds. Better to fill
a red feeder with colorless sugar
water (one part sugar to four parts
water; mix, boil, and cool before
filling). Flowers they like, such as
honeysuckle and trumpet creeper,
will also keep hummers around.

☐ *Check when completed*

❧ TIP 104 ❧

Gardeners are at risk during summer
storms that involve lightning.
Water is a great conductor of
electricity, so get away from the
pool, fountain, sprinklers, and
hose. Don't stand under an oak or
other tall tree, under an arbor,
or in a gazebo. Get in the car,
or get in the house.

❑ *Check when completed*

❧ TIP 105 ❧

Some annuals such as pansies, having exhausted themselves and unable to continue in the summer heat, will quit blooming around now. They are not going to magically revive later. The show is over; yank them out and toss them on the compost pile. Meanwhile, back in the garden, either replace them with fresh reinforcements or mulch over the gap.

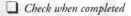

❏ *Check when completed*

❧ TIP 106 ❧

Here's a clever way to water
hanging baskets or other potted
plants, especially when you
won't be around to attend to them
on a hot day. Set a few ice cubes
on their surface before you leave the
house. These will melt slowly
over the course of a few hours,
gradually soaking in.

☐ *Check when completed*

❧ TIP 107 ❧

Are birds eating or pecking
at your developing fruit? Protect the
fruit before it's too late. Drape the
trees with polyester netting—it's
cheap and effective (find it at a
garden supplier in clear or black
mesh). You might have to hold it in
place here and there with an
occasional clothespin.

❏ *Check when completed*

❧ TIP 108 ❧

Mow the lawn less often during dry weather spells. When you do mow, set the mower blades higher to help keep the grass green and allow grass blades to shade out low-growing weeds. (Taller types tend to develop deeper roots.) Don't bother with raking—if you mow often, the clippings will be small enough to break down on site.

❏ *Check when completed*

❧ TIP 109 ❧

Mail-order bulb catalogs will be coming soon. These outlets will afford you a far broader selection of interesting and colorful spring-flowering bulbs than you'd ever see at a garden center, so feast your imagination on the enticing offerings. Order early so you'll get them in time for fall planting.

☐ *Check when completed*

❧ TIP 110 ❧

A whitefly problem can develop
if you have potted plants in
a warm corner of the porch or deck.
One wave of your hand will
send up a cloud of these foliage-
sucking beasties. Fight back with
sprays from the hose. Separate
affected plants, so you can treat
them individually and also to
improve air circulation.

☐ *Check when completed*

❧ TIP III ❧

If you haven't already, clip off
all spent, browned flowers on your
shrubs. They really detract from
the appearance, and they drain
energy from the plant as they
attempt to go to seed. If you don't
do this, they'll hang around all
summer and all winter and detract
from next spring's show.

❑ *Check when completed*

❧ TIP 112 ❧

Flowerbeds looking heat-stressed?
Take a two-pronged approach to
rejuvenation. First, go out in the
morning while it's cool and tidy up,
clipping off spent blooms and
removing bedraggled and excessive
growth. Second, add or renew a
mulch layer at their feet; this helps
retain some soil moisture and
makes the area look neater.

❏ *Check when completed*

❧ TIP 113 ❧

Cut roses for bouquets. Midmorning is ideal because dew has dried but midday heat is not yet depriving the blooms of moisture. Choose buds that are showing color and just beginning to unfurl—these will finish opening indoors, providing you with quite a show. Cut on an angle, underwater if possible, for maximum water uptake.

❑ *Check when completed*

❧ TIP 114 ❧

Pick and dry fragrant herbs—it's
one of gardening's most enchanting
chores. Pick lush stems whose
blossoms have formed but not yet
opened, for maximum scent and
flavor. Rinse them quickly and completely pat dry. Make bundles and
hang them upside-down in a hot,
dark spot, such as an attic. This way,
they'll dry before they can rot.

❏ *Check when completed*

JUNE

❖ TIP 115 ❖

Water the lawn in the early morning. This gives the grass roots time to absorb the moisture before the day's heat steals some due to evaporation. It's also better than afternoon or evening watering because, at those times, moisture can linger and encourage the development of fungal diseases.

❏ *Check when completed*

❖ TIP 116 ❖

Fruit trees ought to be bearing
about this time. Wait till the
color is good before picking. If you
miss the boat and ripe fruit falls
on the ground, snag it right away. It
may be just fine. If you leave it
there, it's only going to rot.

❑ *Check when completed*

❧ TIP 117 ❧

Know when to harvest your green beans. Use the touch test—pick them when you can feel the outlines of the individual seeds in the pod, but not before they start to burst their bounds. Or use the taste test— pick one, right out there in the garden, and take a bite. If it's crunchy and sweet, go for it.

❏ *Check when completed*

❧ TIP 118 ❧

Favorite annuals (gomphrena, zinnias) going to seed? If you like them, let them, and you'll have a crowd next year. But a couple should be reined in, before it's too late, by clipping off their fading flowers or developing seedheads: four o'clocks (self-sown ones never seem to have the same pretty colors) and foxgloves (poisonous to animals).

❑ *Check when completed*

❧ TIP 119 ❧

Lift up and look under your potted
plants. If the contents have been
thriving, roots may have filled the
entire container and be clogging the
drainage holes. If water cannot
drain properly, performance declines
and rot can follow. Two solutions:
repot the contents in something
larger, or remove a plant or two.

☐ *Check when completed*

❦ TIP 120 ❦

If you come outside and observe,
to your horror, that your tomatoes,
peppers, and beans are aborting
their flowers before they ever
have a chance to grow into fruit, do
not panic. This is a common
response to heat stress. Just keep
watering the plants, and they will
become productive again later
in the summer.

❏ *Check when completed*

❧ TIP 121 ❧

Visit the local garden center
while it's not busy to see what's on
sale. While this may not be a
practical time to be buying a lot of
plants, it might be a perfect time to
load up on various pots and
containers, and maybe even some
garden ornaments.

❑ *Check when completed*

❧ TIP 122 ❧

Keep a close watch on your rosebushes. Summer's higher humidity conspires with higher daytime and nighttime temperatures to cause all sorts of fungal disease problems. You can spray preventatively with a fungicide; just follow the label directions carefully, and be sure to work on a windless day.

❑ *Check when completed*

❧ TIP 123 ❧

For the Fourth of July,
make a patriotic flower display. Get
some red or blue pots. Then
fill the red ones with blue and
white annuals, and the blue ones
with red and white flowers.
Group them together—on the front
steps to welcome visitors or to
the side on the patio or deck
where they can be admired.

☐ *Check when completed*

❧ TIP 124 ❧

Dethatch your lawn. Thatch is a
layer of dead grass that builds up at
the soil line, keeping out moisture
and nutrients and leading to decline.
There are special rakes, as well as
power equipment that can help—if
you don't know what you're doing,
hire qualified help.

☐ *Check when completed*

❖ TIP 125 ❖

Help out your potted plants.
Those in clay pots, especially, have
trouble holding onto necessary
moisture. Water in the morning
hours and again in the evening. And
if possible, move them out
of strong light, maybe to a location
under a shady tree.

❑ *Check when completed*

❖ TIP 126 ❖

Pick tomatoes! In many varieties,
the crop can get so heavy that it
pulls down the plant, so you are
doing it a favor by removing weight!
If you have surplus, give it away,
make sauce, or learn how to can.
And remember, garden tomatoes
will change flavor and texture if
they are refrigerated.

❏ *Check when completed*

❧ TIP 127 ❧

The flowers of your summer
bulbs may be past their prime, but
be patient with the leaves. Let them
die down naturally. They are busy
sending valuable starches and sugars
into the root system, to fuel next
year's display. Don't cut off the
leaves until they are completely
yellow and limp.

☐ *Check when completed*

⚜ TIP 128 ⚜

How do you know when
to harvest a cantaloupe? When it's
big? When its skin is colorful?
When you thump it and hear a deep
thud? If these methods sound too
vague, don't worry. Harvest
when the stem slips readily from the
fruit. Pick it up—if the vine falls
away, you are free to walk away
with the cantaloupe.

❏ *Check when completed*

❖ TIP 129 ❖

Time to pick your glads. Make
your move when the first few buds
at the bottom of the spike are
completely open but the rest are
still in bud. (Leave the foliage
on the plant; it replenishes the corm
for next year's show.) Recut the
stems indoors and put them
in a vase of lukewarm water;
change the water daily.

☐ *Check when completed*

❧ TIP 130 ❧

"Solarize" a garden bed in preparation for fall planting. This technique uses the heat of the sun to kill weed seeds and diseases. Dig up the area, till it well, and dampen. Then spread plastic, anchoring the edges with rocks. (Research has shown that clear plastic is more effective than black.) Leave in place for at least a month.

☐ *Check when completed*

❧ TIP 131 ❧

Plant jack-o-lantern pumpkins
(as well as those cute little mini
pumpkins that are so handy for
decorating) now if you want to
harvest by Halloween. Start the
seeds indoors in pots or flats. Cover
them with a thin coating of soil
mix, and place in a warm spot.
They'll germinate quickly.

❏ *Check when completed*

❧ TIP 132 ❧

Later this month, you may plant another round of vegetable seedlings (such as peppers, tomatoes, and cucumbers) for harvest this fall. If it is still far too hot outdoors, nurture the little plants in a bright spot inside until it's safe to move them out.

❏ *Check when completed*

❧ TIP 133 ❧

As soon as flowers or stems
start to turn brown, cut them back
to live growth. This not only
improves their appearance, but helps
prevent insect pests and diseases
from moving in. And it will
encourage some plants to rebloom
later in the season. Cut-and-come-
again favorites include yarrow,
daisies, Russian sage, and phlox.

❑ *Check when completed*

❧ TIP 134 ❧

Clear an area that has been infested by weeds. Hoe or yank out all you can get. Kill the rest and thwart reseeding by treating the bed with a systemic herbicide. Then dig in lots of organic matter and cover the area until you are ready to plant.

❏ *Check when completed*

❧ TIP 135 ❧

Make yourself leave alone those
perennials that are winding down. If
you cut them back too soon or
remove foliage that has not fully
yellowed and fallen over, you are
depriving the root systems of
nutrients that are being passed
down now. Be patient—your reward
will come next year!

❏ *Check when completed*

❧ TIP 136 ❧

Deadhead perennials that are
still generating blooms. This
inspires the plants to keep going.
Also, trim or pinch back the
ends of stems to encourage the
plant to grow a bit more compactly.
You can take out spent inner
branches, though, as these
are no longer productive.

☐ *Check when completed*

❖ TIP 137 ❖

Deter tunneling rodents. Start with
the milder war tactics, such as
flooding the tunnels and setting out
smelly repellents. If that fails, get
some traps. Note that traps that
capture them alive (for release
far from your house!) may or may
not be allowed; check with the
local wildlife officers.

❑ *Check when completed*

❧ TIP 138 ❧

Now is a fine time to attend to your bearded iris plants. Pry up the clump with a garden fork. Cut the foliage low; then split it into clumps, each with some fat rhizomes and a little fan of leaves. Remove iris borers by hand, and discard weak rhizomes. Replant and water— there's time for the divisions to establish before cold weather arrives.

❏ *Check when completed*

❖ TIP 139 ❖

Container roses, including those cute little miniature ones, may still be for sale. Don't plant them in the ground right now. Just keep them in a spot that receives about 6 hours of sun a day, and keep after the water so they don't suffer in the heat. You can put them in the ground later, when cool weather returns.

☐ *Check when completed*

❧ TIP 140 ❧

Before you go on vacation, check
your watering systems very
carefully—even if you have timers
and everything is self-regulating.
(If you have a sophisticated in-
ground system, it would be
worthwhile to call the contractor
who installed it and ask them to
come over for a "tune-up.")

☐ *Check when completed*

❧ TIP 141 ❧

This time of year, always apply
water to the ground within
the drip zone. Doing this not only
delivers water to the roots
more efficiently than overhead
watering, but prevents diseases
that occur when hot weather and
damp foliage collide.

❏ *Check when completed*

❧ TIP 142 ❧

Pick some roses! Cut just as buds are showing color so they can unfurl their beauty—and fragrance—indoors. Take long stems, which you can always shorten when you recut for the vase. If feasible, recut the stems underwater in the sink or a bowl; this florist's trick ensures that the stem is full of water, with no air bubbles.

☐ *Check when completed*

❧ TIP 143 ❧

Thrips on roses are often a
problem this time of year. Telltale
signs include ugly brown spots all
over buds and flowers, and
deformed leaves. Unfortunately, a jet
of water may not be enough to
eradicate them. Try Neem oil or a
pyrethrum-based spray; follow the
label directions very carefully.

☐ *Check when completed*

❧ TIP 144 ❧

Plant Southern peas now; they are well adapted to our climate and will do just fine. Direct-sow them into prepared soil, water regularly, and watch them go! They grow amazingly fast. (If you don't eat them, or eat all of them, you can always till them under to improve the area's organic content.)

☐ *Check when completed*

✦ TIP 145 ✦

Blazing weather slows production in your vegetable garden, but don't despair. Look to the future—buy some seeds for fall planting. Good candidates for July sowing include cabbage, broccoli, and Brussels sprouts. Get them started in flats or small pots of sterile mix in a well-lit (but not hot) spot indoors.

☐ *Check when completed*

❧ TIP 146 ❧

Pick a water lily bouquet!
As you may have noticed, the
blooms last around three
days in a garden pool. And they
do the same in a vase indoors.
They even close up each evening
and reopen each morning. Be sure
to change the water daily.

☐ *Check when completed*

❧ TIP 147 ❧

Done picking blackberries?
Lay the groundwork now for next
year's abundant harvest. Take
a pair of sharp loppers and cut out
all the old canes at ground level—
they're done. Leave all of this
year's green stems, though, as they
will be the ones to bear next
year's flowers and berries.

❏ *Check when completed*

❧ TIP 148 ❧

Protect ripening fruit from
marauding birds. Some or all of the
following tactics are worth a try:
netting made for this purpose,
"metallic" balloons, and strips of
glittering aluminum foil. You can
also harvest a bit early and let the
fruit continue to ripen inside.

❑ *Check when completed*

✤ TIP 149 ✤

Thirsty groundcovers may
need your attention. To maximize
water uptake, irrigate early
on a windless day, and wet the area
to a depth of several inches. Note
that the ones growing in full sun
show their distress sooner, but ones
in shade suffer also.

☐ *Check when completed*

❧ TIP 150 ❧

Bring along a shovel and edit your garden—this is an ideal time to remove plants that didn't work out. Perhaps they took up too much space or didn't perform well, or maybe you simply didn't end up liking the way they look. Dig them up and give them away or toss their remains on the compost pile.

☐ *Check when completed*

❧ TIP 151 ❧

Visit the vegetable garden
and tidy up. Pull out spent plants.
Scoop up plant debris from the
bases of plants that are still growing,
and pinch off dead or yellowing
foliage. Remove and discard
damaged and overripe fruits, from
the plants as well as the ground—
this stuff only encourages
insect pests.

❑ *Check when completed*

❦ TIP 152 ❦

Harvest sunflower seeds—
assuming the birds don't beat you
to it. Cut the flowerhead off with
about a foot of stem attached and
hang it in a dry, airy location to
finish ripening. Whatever you do,
don't stack or bag the heads, or they
will rot. Ripe seeds can be flicked
off and dried further.

☐ *Check when completed*

❧ TIP 153 ❧

This is the month that insect
pests really descend on rosebushes.
Buy don't just spray willy-nilly; get
an accurate identification or
diagnosis and buy the correct
remedy. Also, clean up under the
plants, water at ground level,
and pinch off marred foliage
and spent flowers.

☐ *Check when completed*

❧ TIP 154 ❧

Sow a cover crop in any open spot in need of organic matter. These annuals germinate in cooler, moist soil and may even grow some on milder days. You'll till them under next spring. They will stop erosion and prevent nutrients from leaching away over the winter months. (What kind? Get advice from your local garden center or Extension agent.)

❏ *Check when completed*

❖ TIP 155 ❖

Don't pinch your mums any more now. Let them grow freely so that they will be of substantial size and develop good buds for a colorful fall display. As this process goes forward, remember to keep the plants evenly moist for a better quality flower show.

❑ *Check when completed*

❧ TIP 156 ❧

Rebuild or even expand the
watering basins around the base
of your trees and shrubs, in
anticipation of winter rains. Ideally,
a basin should be as far out as the
"drip line" (furthest extent of the
plant's canopy)—or even a bit
farther. Put compost or another
mulch in the basin.

☐ *Check when completed*

❧ TIP 157 ❧

Prune climbing roses as their blooming slows. Take out old wood, which is gray rather than brown or green. While you're at it, remove some of the stems that bloomed this year, as well as the twiggy growth. Dead, damaged, and diseased wood should also be taken out.

❑ *Check when completed*

❖ TIP 158 ❖

Going on vacation? Find someone to
care for your yard and plants while
you are away—ideally, another
gardener who understands what
needs to be done (watering, mainly).
If you want to try a clever slow-
watering gadget, better try it out
ahead of time to make sure it works.

❏ *Check when completed*

❖ TIP 159 ❖

You can take cuttings of
favorite shrubs—azalea, aucuba,
camellia, Chinese hibiscus, and
euonymus. Take 4- to 6-inch stems,
strip off the lower leaves, dip the
ends in rooting powder, and stick
them in a damp, sandy mix. Cover
with plastic to retain moisture.

☐ *Check when completed*

❧ TIP 160 ❧

Now is the time to renew the organic matter in the tidied-up vegetable garden and in the now-emptied flowerbeds. Well-rotted compost is ideal, or you can buy bagged compost or use dehydrated cow manure. Dig and mix everything to a depth of 6 or more inches.

☐ *Check when completed*

❧ TIP 161 ❧

The best time to harvest
herbs is right before their flowers
open. Their essential oils will
be at their peak now. Examples
include mint, thyme, basil, angelica,
and epazote. Cut in late morning,
after the dew has dried but before
the hot midday sun bakes the
flavor out of the leaves.

❑ *Check when completed*

❧ TIP 162 ❧

Make delicious berry vinegar.
Start with 3 cups of washed, dried
berries (raspberries, blackberries,
even strawberries). Place in a large
ceramic or glass bowl. Heat 4 cups
of plain white vinegar, stir in $1/2$ cup
sugar until dissolved. Pour over
berries, cover and let sit for two
days before straining into
decorative glass bottles.

❏ *Check when completed*

❧ TIP 163 ❧

Shape and trim trees and
shrubs only lightly at this time of
year. For now, the thicker
growth helps protect the trunk and
prevents the lower leaves and
branches from scorching.

☐ *Check when completed*

❧ TIP 164 ❧

Hot weather causes the compost
pile to go into overdrive,
provided you keep it moist. So stop
by with the hose every now and
then and give it a soaking. Then stir,
using a long stick or a tool
handle. Adding nitrogen, organic
fertilizers, coffee grounds, or tea
leaves seems to help accelerate
the decomposition activity.

☐ *Check when completed*

❧ TIP 165 ❧

Summer-blooming wildflowers
are going to seed. Clip them off and
dry them, collecting the seeds for
future use. Store them in a cool, dry,
dark place so they don't germinate
too soon. Plan to sow them later in
the fall or early next year—write
yourself a reminder.

❑ *Check when completed*

❖ TIP 166 ❖

Yellow jackets can be a big problem
now out in the yard. Sudden
movements can provoke them, and
they love moisture-beaded cans
of soft drinks. Whatever you do,
don't squish one, because it releases
a scent that draws more yellow
jackets. Brush them away slowly, and
retreat. Treat nests late in the
evening with hornet/wasp spray.

❏ *Check when completed*

❧ TIP 167 ❧

Examine the base of your fruit
trees. If suckers are originating from
the rootstock, the trees will never
produce viable fruit. Cut them away,
using a sharp pair of clippers or
loppers. A callus will develop, so it
is not necessary to paint
over the wound.

❑ *Check when completed*

❧ TIP 168 ❧

Rein in your aggressive vines.
Those that are growing on the side
of the house or up a porch pillar can
all too easily insinuate themselves
into woodwork and windows. Chop
back excessive growth now.
Common culprits include trumpet
creeper, Virginia creeper, euonymus,
and English ivy.

❑ *Check when completed*

❧ TIP 169 ❧

Annuals that have been blooming all summer may now be running out of steam. Others, such as angelonias, calibrachoas, and petunias, can be revived and persuaded to make an encore performance if you clip them back and keep on watering. All the rest, sadly, ought to come out and be sent to the compost pile.

☐ *Check when completed*

❧ TIP 170 ❧

Coleus plants, in the ground or in pots, are real troopers! Reward their hard work by continuing to give them good care. Pinch off their tops from time to time to encourage bushy growth. Clear away debris from the bases of the plants. Water regularly and deeply.

❏ *Check when completed*

❧ TIP 171 ❧

Water your rosebushes—do not neglect them. Deliver the water at the bases of the plants, though, as damp leaves are susceptible to disease. They should be ramping up for a big September and October show, and you want them to be well hydrated so they can deliver.

☐ *Check when completed*

❧ TIP 172 ❧

Go mum shopping. The garden centers should be getting their plants out about this time, and the earlier you get there, the more choices you'll have. Look for new and more vivid colors—the plant breeders are always making improvements and bringing out new introductions.

❏ *Check when completed*

❖ TIP 173 ❖

You don't have to pull out fading tomato plants. Try this: chop them back drastically, to about a foot tall. Continue to water and care for them as fall approaches. They often respond by putting out new growth—and, later in the fall, a respectable harvest.

☐ *Check when completed*

❖ TIP 174 ❖

Some fall bloomers will not form
buds, and thus turn in a
disappointing performance, if you
do not water them now. Asters,
mums, and dahlias are classic
examples. Irrigate them often—and
consistently. Verify that the water is
actually reaching the root zone by
digging down to check.

❏ *Check when completed*

❖ TIP 175 ❖

Orchids that have finished
blooming will want a rest. Floral
stalks that turn brown all the
way back to the main stem are spent
and can be clipped off. If the
plant put on a lot of growth and
now looks dense or crowded,
you can repot.

☐ *Check when completed*

❧ TIP 176 ❧

Check on your rain barrel.
Empty any lingering water
somewhere it can be used. Then
scrub out the interior with a stiff
brush to remove any algae or other
crud. Return it to its spot and be
sure to cover it with a screen to keep
out debris and bugs. Fall rains
should soon refill it.

❑ *Check when completed*

❧ TIP 177 ❧

If you are a collards greens fan, now is the time to make your move. Prepare an area for sowing. Then dig in some lime and fertilizer. Broadcast the seeds shallowly, and moisten the area. To prevent insect problems, shelter the developing seedlings under a row cover.

☐ *Check when completed*

❖ TIP 178 ❖

Shrub roses and old-fashioned varieties often develop bright and attractive fruits called "rose hips." If you like the look (or if you want to harvest them to make a tea rich in Vitamin C), stop deadheading these bushes—that will give the hips a chance to develop.

❏ *Check when completed*

❧ TIP 179 ❧

Plan your fall flowerbeds on paper.
Make yourself do this before you
peek at the nursery catalogs, so you
don't "put the cart before the horse."
Your plan may be an informal
picture on regular or graph paper,
but try to make it to scale.
Gardening books and nursery
catalogs will help you with mature-
plant size estimates.

☐ *Check when completed*

❖ TIP 180 ❖

Spend a little time on your rosebushes, with the aims of not only improving their looks but preventing insect and disease problems. Get rid of yellowed or diseased leaves. Clean up any that have fallen on the ground under the plants. Spray for blackspot and powdery mildew.

❑ *Check when completed*

❧ Everyday Tip ❧

Visit a public garden, or go on a
garden tour. Bring your camera and,
just as important, a notebook.
With or without the help of a guide,
you will find plenty to learn and lots
of inspiration. Be sure to write
down the names of plants or plant
combinations you admire (if there
are no labels, ask someone).

It's time to feed the tall fescue lawn. Use a fertilizer that is high in nitrogen, the element that nourishes stems and root growth. Remember to water the lawn before and after applying the fertilizer; apply at the rates recommended on the label, and no more.

☐ *Check when completed*

❦ TIP 182 ❦

Prepare or rejuvenate planting beds. Pull out plants that have faded, and get rid of all the weeds. Then dig in some organic matter to a depth of 6 or more inches (compost is perfect). Rake over lightly; then mulch the surface until you are ready to add plants.

❏ *Check when completed*

❧ TIP 183 ❧

Go shopping for garden mums.
Avoid the temptation to
buy ones that are already blooming,
because chances are the trip
home in the hot car or the process
of transplanting (or both) will
simply cause them to drop their
petals. Instead, buy ones that
are full of buds.

❑ *Check when completed*

❧ TIP 184 ❧

Ramp up the fall vegetable garden. Begin by removing the remnants of the spring and summer crops. It is very important not just to remove these plants but to get out fallen leaves and fruit from them as well, since these might be harboring diseases. Then scoop on lots of organic matter, several inches' worth, and mix and dig well.

❑ *Check when completed*

❧ TIP 185 ❧

If you have a cold frame, or have
been thinking of making one,
fall is a good time to build one.
Little seedlings can be raised and
acclimated in its shelter. You can
also order one already to assemble
from garden catalogs.

❑ *Check when completed*

❧ TIP 186 ❧

Start favorite vegetables for the fall garden. Salad and mustard greens can be sown directly. Others can be started ahead of time indoors or purchased as seedlings down at the garden center—broccoli, cauliflower, cabbage, and the like.

❑ *Check when completed*

❧ TIP 187 ❧

The single most important nutrient your fruit trees need heading into winter is potassium. Supply it with greensand, wood ash, or sulfate potash. Ask at your local nursery for the material, as well as the recommended rates for the types of trees you have and their age.

☐ *Check when completed*

❧ TIP 188 ☙

Ripening peppers ought to be left on the plant as long as possible. The warm days and cool nights of fall inspire a good fruit set and excellent flavor. Take only what you need for tonight's meal. If you are an impatient harvester, you can bring some in and let them finish ripening in a warm kitchen.

❑ *Check when completed*

❖ TIP 189 ❖

Keep an eye on your lawn and be ready to mow again as needed. Lawn grass slows growth in hot spells and resumes when the weather cools down. Meanwhile, don't deprive it of water—but don't overdo either. Deliver about an inch of water every few days, or whenever the grass looks wilted.

❏ *Check when completed*

❧ TIP 190 ❧

If you have the bigger, rangy boxwoods, give them an autumn trim. Take a bit off all sides as well as the top; this inspires thicker growth lower down, giving the plants a more compact and lush look. Do this before mid-September in most areas—any later, and you run the risk of that new growth getting cold-damage.

❑ *Check when completed*

❧ TIP 191 ❧

Tour the yard with a pair of sharp loppers and good clippers, now that the summer heat is dissipating. Take out branches that are obviously dead, dying, or damaged—they're not going to recover. Just this simple operation helps your plants look much better and benefits their overall health.

❏ *Check when completed*

❧ TIP 192 ❧

Do you feel like your autumn
landscape lacks color and punch?
Visit a public garden, nursery, or
arboretum to find out what is
looking fabulous right now in your
area. Perhaps you can plant
something this year; if not, make a
wish list and act on it next spring.

❑ *Check when completed*

❧ TIP 193 ❧

Cut fragrant flowers early in the day
while they are full of moisture.
Scent resides within the cells of the
petals, so the higher the water
content, the higher the amount of
scent ingredient. Prolong the delight
by displaying them in a vase that is
set in indirect or low light.

☐ *Check when completed*

❧ TIP 194 ❧

Lay the groundwork for a bountiful herb harvest later in the year. In a bright, sunny spot—ideally, not far from your kitchen—create a raised bed or prepare various pots with well-drained, organically rich soil. Fill with seedlings of parsley, sage, oregano, thyme, chives, and cilantro.

❑ *Check when completed*

❧ TIP 195 ❧

Certain vegetables can be sown directly into the vegetable garden right about now, and they will produce a good harvest well before the really cold weather arrives. The best choices are edible-root crops such as carrots, radishes, and turnips. Remember, regular watering is the key.

❑ *Check when completed*

❧ TIP 196 ❧

Go shopping and treat yourself
to a new pair of gardening gloves!
Try them on first to be sure
they are comfortable and that you
can move your fingers and
wrists easily. If you are really in the
mood to splurge, get calfskin
ones—they'll serve you well
for years to come.

❏ *Check when completed*

❖ TIP 197 ❖

You may plant lilies now: true
lilies (*Lilium*) as well as
rain lilies and spider lilies. A broad
selection of types and colors
are waiting for you down at the
garden center. Just be sure
you plant them in good, well-
drained soil in a sunny spot.

❑ *Check when completed*

❧ # TIP 198 ❧

Sow wildflower and meadow mixes now for a sensational show next spring. Be wary of ones that are not labeled specifically for your region. Look out for high grasses content, as this is basically filler. In all cases, the label should provide basic planting instructions.

☐ *Check when completed*

❧ TIP 199 ❧

As the air and water temperatures drop, aquatic plants in a garden pond will begin to go dormant. Hardy ones can be cut back and lowered into the deepest water to overwinter; tropical ones should also get a "haircut," but may be safest overwintered inside.

❑ *Check when completed*

❧ TIP 200 ❧

Plant some lavender today!
The plants like plentiful sun and
lean, gravelly soil. Instead of
mulching with compost or
bark chips, which trap moisture
around their crowns, spread pebbles
at their feet. This helps moisture
drain away and keeps your lavender
plants quite happy.

❑ *Check when completed*

❧ TIP 201 ❧

Autumn is a good time to
lay sod. Get rid of the old grass, as
well as weeds, roots, and rocks.
Till lightly to loosen the soil,
sprinkle a little lawn fertilizer
(follow the amount directions on
the bag), and rake smooth.
Work on a cool, cloudy day, and
water the fresh sod well.

☐ *Check when completed*

❦ TIP 202 ❦

Depending on your area, you
may feed your rosebushes now, for
what is likely the last time
this year. If it hasn't rained, be sure
to soak the soil before and after
applying the fertilizer. Use a product
labeled especially for roses, and
follow the directions carefully—
more is not better.

❏ *Check when completed*

❧ TIP 203 ❧

Harvest and cure onions. While they're still in the ground, knock over their tops with a rake. Make your move a week later—get them out of the ground, wipe free of dirt, and array on screens to dry. Only then can you clip off their tops. Store in a cold, dry place.

❑ *Check when completed*

❖ TIP 204 ❖

Plant some peonies! These beautiful, tough perennials relish organically rich soil. The only tricky part is placing them at the proper planting depth—the little pink "eyes" (buds) on their clumping roots should end up no more than 2 inches below the soil surface.

☐ *Check when completed*

❧ TIP 205 ❧

If leaves are falling, start raking. If
you wait till they all drop, the job
can be too big! Scoot piles off
to one side or stuff them in paper
bags as you work. You can compost
them or use them as a mulch
(chopped up, preferably—run over
them with the lawn mower).

❑ *Check when completed*

❖ TIP 206 ❖

Shop the sales at the garden center.
Perennials, ornamental grasses, even
rosebushes, may be offered at
bargain prices. If it's still too hot to
plant, hold these in their pots
in a sheltered location for a couple
of weeks. Just remember to stop by
often, even daily, to see if they
need a drink of water.

❏ *Check when completed*

❧ TIP 207 ❧

Save yourself a big and messy
clean-up job by laying netting over
your garden pool now. If fall leaves
land on its surface, they'll clog it,
suffocate plants and fish, decay, and
will generally be a nuisance. The
netting will also discourage
animals and birds.

☐ *Check when completed*

❖ TIP 208 ❖

Time to tuck in some color
in the garden gaps. Nurseries and
garden centers will have plenty
of sedums, and ornamental kales
and cabbages for sale. These are
favorites, with good reason. They're
durable and long-lasting, and as
temperatures drop, their color often
gets richer. Mums are also offered in
a rainbow of hues—mix and match!

❏ *Check when completed*

❧ TIP 209 ❧

Cut your dahlias as often as you can. The more you harvest, the more the plants will produce—you can't say that about every flower, but dahlias never disappoint. Just be sure you have a tall and sturdy vase (something tilt-proof!) to hold them, because some varieties are quite big and top-heavy.

❏ *Check when completed*

❧ TIP 210 ❧

Plant garlic as the nights cool down. Fertile soil is important, but even more important is well drained soil, lest your bulbs rot in soggy ground. (Growing garlic in a raised bed works great.) Plant individual cloves an inch deep, pointed end up, and mulch well. Most aboveground growth won't occur till spring.

☐ *Check when completed*

❧ Tip 211 ❧

Find out your area's predicted
first fall frost date. Check your local
paper, or call a garden center or
nearby Cooperative Extension
office. Though it's usually not till
later this month or November,
depending on where you live, you
need to know now so you can
calculate how much gardening
time you have left.

❏ *Check when completed*

❧ TIP 212 ❧

Plant herbs. They will grow quickly in the still-warm soil, watered in by fall rains, and be ready to use in a month or two. That's good timing if you like to use fresh herbs in holiday cooking or want to harvest some for gift-giving.

❏ *Check when completed*

❧ TIP 213 ❧

Try raising your own salad mix!
Seed companies call these blends
"mesclun," and they often contain a
range of lettuces, as well as other
tasty edible leafy greens. Sow in
moist, well-drained soil, and lay
down a row cover (it shields them
from a late frost, plant pests, and
hot sun). They grow rapidly.

❑ *Check when completed*

❧ TIP 214 ❧

Hot days and cool nights can
cause tomatoes to develop unsightly
splits in the sides of the fruit. If you
are worried this is going to happen,
try to moderate the effects by
keeping the plants evenly moist.
Also, don't leave tomatoes on the
vine too long—harvest them as soon
as you see early signs of marring.

❏ *Check when completed*

❧ TIP 215 ❧

Time to start bringing tender and tropical potted plants inside. Give them one last good watering outside, and check thoroughly for insect pests. Groom the plants, and cut off all remaining flower stalks and scraggly foliage. Find them a cool, nonfreezing spot, such as a screened-in porch or sunroom.

❑ *Check when completed*

❧ TIP 216 ❧

Plant a shrub or tree. The soil is still warm, and drenching fall rains will help water it in. Dig an ample hole, and mix native soil with some organic matter for backfilling. Set the plant in at the level it was growing in the pot, and press the dirt firmly around it. Water weekly until the ground freezes.

☐ *Check when completed*

❧ TIP 217 ❧

Protect your ripening pumpkins.
About now, the skin should be hard
and the color should be darkening,
but if they are exposed to a light
frost, they can turn black—what a
disappointment. Just cover the plant
with a tarp for the night if the
forecast is for cold temperatures.

❑ *Check when completed*

❧ TIP 218 ❧

Now is the time to plant seedlings of cool-season vegetables. They relish both organically rich soil and the cooler fall temperatures. If you keep them well watered and feed them (side-dress with an all-purpose or organic fertilizer), your cool-season vegetables will be wonderfully productive.

❏ *Check when completed*

❧ TIP 219 ❧

Plant cool-season annuals for a
boost of late color. There will be lots
to choose from at the garden centers
right now. Bright selections include
calendula, snapdragons, and pansies.
If you poke around a bit, you may
find these in new colors or
bicolors—those plant breeders are
always busy trying to dazzle us.

☐ *Check when completed*

❧ TIP 220 ❧

Are daylilies overcrowded and
blooming more sparsely? Divide
them now to jumpstart your spring
display. Prepare the new bed or area
first, though, so the roots won't dry
out. Dig up the clumps, and divide
into sections (back-to-back gardening forks might be needed). Replant
husky pieces that include a good
chunk of roots and topgrowth.

❑ *Check when completed*

❖ TIP 221 ❖

If rain is not regular or abundant this month, you are going to have to step in and provide supplemental water. Don't wait until the shrubs and flowering plants are wilting or showing other signs of distress. Soak regularly and consistently so they remain healthy and strong—better able to withstand the coming winter, as well as pests and diseases.

❏ *Check when completed*

❧ TIP 222 ❧

Plant some evergreens—hollies,
yews, boxwoods, or junipers. Find
them at the nursery in large
containers. Prepare a hole that is as
deep and as wide than the rootball.
Mix in some organic matter with
the native soil, and use this
improved blend to backfill.

☐ *Check when completed*

❖ TIP 223 ❖

Buying bulbs locally? Examine each one. It should be clean, with no blemishes. Squeeze it to be sure it is firm and plump. Compare it to its fellows and choose the heftier ones (light ones are dried up inside). Note that comparatively bigger ones have more stored reserves and thus are more likely to put on a big show.

☐ *Check when completed*

❧ TIP 224 ❧

Feed your trees and shrubs one last time. At this point in the year, shoot growth has ceased and the still actively growing roots of woody plants will make most efficient use of the fertilizer's nutrients. Research has shown that early spring growth depends heavily on this stored bounty.

❏ *Check when completed*

❖ TIP 225 ❖

Have you admired those random, bright, and colorful drifts of spring bulbs, but wondered how to get that spontaneous "naturalized" look? It's easy. Just toss handfuls into the chosen area and plant each one where it lands. Dig a hole twice as deep as the bulb's size, sprinkle in some compost, set in the bulb, cover, and water.

❏ *Check when completed*

❖ TIP 226 ❖

Keep raking fall leaves. If you
wait till they all drop, the job can be
too big! Scoot piles off to one side
or stuff them in paper bags as you
work. You can compost them or use
them as a mulch (chopped up,
preferably—run over them with
the lawn mower).

❑ *Check when completed*

❧ TIP 227 ❧

Prune your roses. Approach the project in three main steps: First, take out all "nonnegotiable" growth first (dead or diseased wood, damaged canes); second, thin the plant by removing rubbing and crossing branches; finally, shape the bush by removing small amounts of growth all around.

❑ *Check when completed*

❧ TIP 228 ❧

Planting depth for bulbs varies by type, but the general rule of thumb is twice as deep as they are high. If you are digging individual holes, make them ample and push some compost into the bottom of the hole to nurture the developing roots. Apply bulb fertilizer to the soil surface afterwards.

☐ *Check when completed*

❦ TIP 229 ❦

Fertilize the lawn. It's much
smarter to do this now, rather than
in the spring (when the food would
also inspire a fresh growth spurt
from weeds!). Topgrowth is slowing
down or finished, so the nutrients
will fortify the roots. Remember
to water before and after for
the best uptake.

❑ *Check when completed*

❖ TIP 230 ❖

Fertilize bulb plantings with care. If you mix the plant food into the bed, it can burn tender roots at a time when they don't need any stress. Instead, "top-dress" bulbs by sprinkling it on the surface and watering it in. Granular Holland Bulb Booster™ (9-9-6) is great for tulips and other favorites.

❑ *Check when completed*

❧ TIP 231 ❧

Gather a colorful fall arrangement.
Start with a few branches of vivid
fall foliage. Fill in with softer
textured but bright fall perennials
such as goldenrod and purple
asters. Add a few branches that are
adorned with red berries or red
rose hips (strip foliage from these).
Use the seedheads of ornamental
grasses as dramatic filler.

☐ *Check when completed*

❖ TIP 232 ❖

Haul the hose or sprinkler out to the camellia or gardenia bed and give it a thorough drenching. It should head into the winter months well watered. Otherwise, cold weather may cause the leaves to "burn" or develop dry edges. As the saying goes, "An ounce of prevention . . ."

❑ *Check when completed*

❧ TIP 233 ❧

If the soil can still be worked, plant perennial types of onions (bunching onions, shallots). They don't need special care; just give them a spot with decent soil and they'll be fine. Water them deeply only if rainfall is sparse. In a few weeks, they'll develop leafy tops that also happen to be tasty.

❑ *Check when completed*

❧ TIP 234 ❧

Save the seeds that you scoop
out of your Halloween jack-o-
lantern. Spread them out and dry
them on a tray or paper plate, then
put them out for the birds. A
platform bird feeder displays and
holds them well. Cardinals in
particular relish this treat.

❑ *Check when completed*

❖ TIP 235 ❖

Remove suckers from your apple
and crabapple trees—suckers both
divert energy from the tree and
detract from its appearance. Gently
digging down to the source of the
sucker, with your fingers or a trowel,
will provide more complete removal
than just lopping it off.

☐ *Check when completed*

❖ TIP 236 ❖

Stop fertilizing the garden around now. A dose of plant food only inspires a flush of new, green growth, and with cold weather coming, you don't want that. Fresh new growth is notoriously vulnerable to frost damage. Store the fertilizers in a cool, dry place for the winter.

❑ *Check when completed*

❧ TIP 237 ❧

Continue to mow the lawn as long as it is growing. Don't scalp it, but do keep it looking neat. This sends it into winter looking as good as can be expected and means it will be in better shape next spring when growth ramps up again.

❑ *Check when completed*

❧ TIP 238 ❧

Harvest remaining leafy greens. The flavor tends to be lighter in young ones and hotter or more intense in older ones, so make your move according to your personal taste. In any event, never cut more than you can use right away. Flavor and vitamin levels tend to dissipate in refrigerated greens.

❏ *Check when completed*

❧ TIP 239 ❧

Bring some herbs in for the winter.
Cut them back to live growth first.
Then dig them up and put them in
pots, watering well. Leave the pots
in a sheltered area for a while,
checking on them from time to
time, just to get them used to
container life. Move them indoors
when frost threatens.

❑ *Check when completed*

❧ TIP 240 ❧

Create a winter lawn. Sow perennial ryegrass; garden centers and supply stores should have the seed. Follow the directions on the side of the bag regarding how much is needed for the area you want to fill. Water in well so it gets off to a good start.

❑ *Check when completed*

Are deer an ongoing problem?
Their destructive dining can be even
more frustrating this time of year,
when they go after young, emerging
plants or ones you've just installed.
Various repellents can work, but if
those deer are relentless and you
mean business, you need an 8-foot-
tall fence around your garden.

☐ *Check when completed*

❧ TIP 242 ❧

Buy fertilizer now—not to use,
but to stockpile. The fall planting
season has wound down, and
the holiday merchandise will soon
be arriving. That means merchants
are eager to unload supplies that
are taking up space. Store plant
food in a cool, dry place until
needed next spring.

☐ *Check when completed*

❧ TIP 243 ❧

Watch for bugs that try to enter
your home or garage looking for
shelter and warmth. Common
culprits include ladybugs and
box elder bugs. They won't harm
wood, pets, or you, but they
are a nuisance. Your best bet
is to thwart them with caulking
and weather-stripping.

❑ *Check when completed*

❧ TIP 244 ❧

Buy amaryllis bulbs right now, if
you want them to be part of your
late-winter or holiday season décor.
They typically take six to eight
weeks to bloom. Get prepotted
"kits," or buy loose bulbs and pot
them yourself. Just remember
that the hefty bulb should be set
half-in, half-out of the mix.

❏ *Check when completed*

❖ TIP 245 ❖

For an early spring harvest in milder winter areas, you can grow some leafy herbs. Some good candidates include parsley, chervil, and coriander. Prepare pots or a small bed with loose, well-drained soil, then direct-sow the seeds. Cover them with a thin layer of soil and water. They'll sprout quickly.

❑ *Check when completed*

❧ TIP 246 ❧

Assuming the ground is warm enough, you can still plant or move around spring-blooming bulbs, particularly tough daffodils. Just give each bulb an ample hole to which you have added some organic matter. Don't plant too deeply— twice as deep as the height of the bulb is just fine.

❑ *Check when completed*

❧ TIP 247 ❧

Cut back your taller perennials
before frost comes—even if there's
some lingering live growth, flowers,
or seedheads. Chopping down to
within a few inches above the soil
level seems brutal, but it will do no
harm and the way will be cleared for
next spring's resurgence.

☐ *Check when completed*

NOVEMBER

❖ TIP 248 ❖

Spare a few perennials whose
dried flowers have winter value.
Birds may enjoy the dried
flowerheads, either as a place to
alight or a seed source. And
whenever snow finally arrives, some
of these plants look beautiful with a
jaunty white cap. Examples include:
ornamental grasses, echinacea,
sedum, rudbeckia, and astilbe.

❏ *Check when completed*

❖ TIP 249 ❖

Time to close down the
vegetable garden. Pull out and
compost all plant debris, with the
exception of anything that was
diseased (bag up that stuff and send
it away with the household trash).
Mulch with chopped-up fall leaves
or compost (or both), which you
can dig in next spring.

☐ *Check when completed*

❖ TIP 250 ❖

Mulch your perennial beds.
Scoop and shovel on plenty of
mulch, to a depth of several inches
or until the chopped-off crowns of
the plants are out of view. Mulch
protects the root systems over the
coming cold months, preventing
frost-heaving and moderating soil-
temperature fluctuations.

❑ *Check when completed*

❖ TIP 251 ❖

Empty all the windowboxes
now, when you finally have time.
Discard the soil mix, as well
as the dead plants. Scrub them out a
bit with a brush, and wipe them
down inside and out. It doesn't take
long, and you'll be glad you did
this when spring returns and you get
in the mood to refill them.

❏ *Check when completed*

❧ TIP 252 ❧

Move emptied pots and containers
of all kinds in out of the weather.
Rinse them out if they're dirty,
and stack them in the garage, shed,
or basement. Instead of getting rid
of cracked clay pots, break them
into small pieces and save these;
they may come in handy for a
drainage layer another day.

❑ *Check when completed*

❖ TIP 253 ❖

Make a pre-emptive strike on winter weeds. Apply a post-emergent herbicide; make sure you get the correct product for the sort of weeds that plague your lawn and garden. Apply according to the directions, and keep in mind that more is not better. Rain ought to water it in. Otherwise, you should.

❏ *Check when completed*

❧ TIP 254 ❧

If you expect the ground to freeze, dig up gladiolus corms and dahlia tubers. Dry them on screens for a day or two, and then clean them off. Store them in bags in a frost-free spot. Don't forget to label! And sprinkle a little fungicide dust into each bag to prevent rot.

❑ *Check when completed*

❧ TIP 255 ❧

Go out and take a very careful look at your camellia bushes. This is the time of year when tea scale can become a problem. Pick off and dispose of affected stems and leaves, if there are only a few. If the infestation is severe, spray the plant with dormant oil.

❏ *Check when completed*

Brown or rotted spots on your African violet leaves? This is an easy problem to solve. It comes from moisture getting on their fuzzy surface. That's why the best way to water these is from the bottom. Just set the pot in a saucer of water and let it wick up what it needs.

❑ *Check when completed*

❧ TIP 257 ❧

It's time to put away the
hummingbird feeders. Clean
them thoroughly with
hot, soapy water and pack
away until next year.

❑ *Check when completed*

Browse the gardening section in your favorite bookstore. New gardening books are often issued this time of year, just before the holiday season. If you don't buy a title for yourself, at least you can make a "wish list" and place hints for friends and relatives.

☐ *Check when completed*

❧ TIP 259 ❧

Close up the compost pile for the winter. Its activity has been slowing for a while now, and tossing kitchen scraps on it at this point leads only to a pile of chilly or frozen garbage that doesn't break down. Give it one last stir, if possible; then replace the lid or cover it with a tarp to discourage rodents.

❑ *Check when completed*

❧ TIP 260 ❧

Protect marginally hardy rosebushes. The grafted ones, in particular, have a hard time in cold weather and can die down to the rootstock (thus the roses you wanted are killed off). Shovel mulch over the base of the plant, up and over the bulging graft.

❏ *Check when completed*

❖ TIP 261 ❖

Attend a winter gardening class
or an interesting lecture. Flyers
for these will be at garden centers,
listed in local newspapers, or
described in the newsletters of
nearby botanic gardens or arboreta.
Or surf the Internet. It's good to get
out of the house—and always
worthwhile to get educated and
inspired in the off-season.

❑ *Check when completed*

❧ TIP 262 ❧

Shorter days with less light inspire spider plants to form "spiders" at last. Let these grow to several inches big, then sever them from the mother plant and pot up. Nurture them in a warm, bright room for now; don't neglect watering. Later, you can move them into their own hanging basket or give them away.

❑ *Check when completed*

❧ TIP 263 ❧

You may plant some spring-blooming bulbs now. If you like tulips, seek out more offbeat kinds, like fluted "parrot" ones or ones with fringed petals. If you like daffodils, look for the pink-cupped ones, or smaller-flowered but highly fragrant white ones. Just for fun, purchase something offbeat, like orange or yellow fritillary.

❏ *Check when completed*

❖ TIP 264 ❖

If you haven't already done so, cover the grill and your lawn furniture for the winter. Or bring them into a protected area inside, such as the garage or basement. If you leave these things exposed to the elements for many months, no matter how durable they are, there's likely to be damage or fading.

❑ *Check when completed*

❧ TIP 265 ❧

Clean your outdoor cushions. Use a stiff brush to get off dirt; then whack out the dust. Put them to dry in a warm area for several days, such as the laundry room (better still, if they will fit, run them through the dryer). There must be absolutely no lingering moisture, or they will mildew or become smelly in storage.

❏ *Check when completed*

❧ TIP 266 ❧

Move houseplants that spent the summer outside off the sun porch or other suddenly chilly area. They will be better off in a warmer winter home, such as a windowsill. South-facing windows are ideal if the plants need maximum light. (Remove the screens from these windows for the winter—it does increase light slightly.)

❑ *Check when completed*

✤ TIP 267 ✤

Drain the hose and bring it in
for the winter. Wipe down its
surface with a cloth so there's no
moisture or mud. Don't hang
it. Store it flat, someplace dry and
dark. Let it coil the way it does
naturally; forcing it in other ways,
especially when it is cold,
leads to cracks.

❏ *Check when completed*

❧ TIP 268 ❧

Clean off caked-on dirt and mud
from shovels and other large
implements before putting them
away for the winter. Fill a bucket
with sand and mix in some
vegetable oil until it's moistened.
Plunge in the blade of each dirty
tool. The sand's abrasion will help
clean it off and the oil will coat
the tool, which prevents rust.

❑ *Check when completed*

❧ TIP 269 ❧

Save fireplace ashes, assuming you burn regular hardwood logs, not anything with additives. Just scoop them into a bag or bucket and reserve them in a dry place. These can be used in the spring as a soil amendment. They offer potash and lime for your plants.

☐ *Check when completed*

❧ TIP 270 ❧

Buy some bales of straw or hay to stockpile for winter mulching. Straw has fewer weed seeds than regular hay. Just pile this off to the side someplace and raid it as needed in the coming weeks. It's so much easier to have it on hand right when you need it!

☐ *Check when completed*

❧ EVERYDAY TIP ❧

You don't have to be a Latin
scholar, but it helps to learn the
basics of the scientific plant
naming system. The first word
(italic and always capitalized) is the
genus, and the second word
is the species. If there is another
word set off by single quotation
marks, then that is a specific variety
sometimes called a cultivar.

❧ TIP 271 ❧

Evaluate your vegetable garden and make notes for next year; tuck these notes where you can refer to them early next spring. Do you need more space for ramblers like squash, zucchini, and pumpkin? Did you have too many tomato plants and not enough peppers? Should the entire garden be bigger or smaller?

☐ *Check when completed*

❧ TIP 272 ❧

Protect the young trees in
your yard from small rodents,
rabbits, and deer that nibble during
the winter. If they "girdle" the tree
(strip away or destroy bark either
part or all the way around), it can
die. Thwart these pests by putting a
cylinder of hardware cloth around
each tree and pressing it into the
ground a few inches.

❑ *Check when completed*

❧ TIP 273 ❧

Draft an overall "wish list" of
your garden goals. Is it to have more
cut flowers, reduce mowing time
or incorporate a major redesign?
Then, plan how to make your goals
a reality, both design-wise and
financially, if it's a big project.

☐ *Check when completed*

❧ TIP 274 ❧

Make some durable plant labels,
while you have time and are
thinking of it. Then just stash them
away until next spring. You won't
get everything taken care of, of
course, but you can certainly do
ones for major, favorite plants. Write
on metal markers with a grease
pencil or on smooth rocks with a
permanent marker.

❏ *Check when completed*

❧ TIP 275 ❧

Place poinsettia plants wisely, so they will look good as long as possible. A windowsill location that gets six hours of light per day is ideal. Avoid drafty areas and temperatures under 70 degrees Fahrenheit or so. A spot close to a heat source, however, dries out the plant and causes the flowers (actually, colorful bracts) to fade.

☐ *Check when completed*

❖ TIP 276 ❖

On a mild day, tour the yard and look closely for signs of frost heaving. Freeze-thaw cycles cause entire plant rootballs, especially of newer plants and shrubs, to rise above the ground, sometimes at alarmingly crooked angles. Just push the plants back into place, and mulch or remulch them to prevent it from happening again.

☐ *Check when completed*

❦ TIP 277 ❦

Fertilize winter ryegrass lawn monthly. Use a high-nitrogen lawn food labeled for this use and apply according to the directions on the bag—you don't want to overdo, just keep it growing and in good health. Water thoroughly at this time, too, for best results.

☐ *Check when completed*

❧ TIP 278 ❧

Protect garden concrete—such as pots, urns, and birdbaths—from winter damage. Because it absorbs water that can freeze, concrete cracks all too easily. Waterproof those prized items with a silicon-based water seal, a paint meant for outdoor use, or even a thin layer of white cement. At least, cover or turn over vulnerable pieces.

❑ *Check when completed*

❖ TIP 279 ❖

Protect young and cold-sensitive
plants out in the yard if
frost threatens. The growing tip is
the most vulnerable part of the
plant and is easily shielded—just
cover it with a large grocery
store paper bag. Remove it later,
after the danger is over.

❑ *Check when completed*

❧ TIP 280 ❧

Clean dusty houseplant leaves.
Not only is the coating unattractive,
but it inhibits the exchange of air
and moisture for the plant, which
can be bad for its health. Wipe
them with a soapy sponge, and then
rinse with clear water. Dust and
dirt can be brushed off textured or
fuzzy leaves with a paintbrush or
clean make-up brush.

❑ *Check when completed*

❧ TIP 281 ❧

Decorate an outdoor tree to attract hungry overwintering birds. Drape it with garlands made of popcorn, cranberries, peanuts still in their shells, raisins, and bits of orange peel. Hang carrots, apples, colorful Indian corn, and chunks of suet. As the saying goes, "If you build it, they will come!"

❏ *Check when completed*

❧ TIP 282 ❧

Make ornaments from pinecones.
Bring them indoors a few days
ahead of time, and set them in a
warm place. This dries them out
completely, evicts lingering
bugs, and ensures that they are fully
open. Roll them in household glue
and dust them with colorful
sequins or glitter. Fashion loops
from ribbons or yarn.

☐ *Check when completed*

❦ TIP 283 ❦

If you haven't done so already,
service the lawn mower.
Clean off the entire surface, above
and below. Then drain the gas,
change the oil, and sharpen the
blades before returning the machine
to storage. You'll be congratulating
yourself for taking the time now
when you need it to be in top
running condition come spring.

❏ *Check when completed*

❧ TIP 284 ❧

The "off" season is a good
opportunity to increase
your plant knowledge. Check out
the local opportunities for
community college classes. Usually,
the next semester or quarter
begins in January.

❑ *Check when completed*

❧ TIP 285 ❧

Make a wreath from evergreen
cuttings in your own yard.
Visit a hobby store and buy a round
wire base, green plastic tape, and
green florist's wire. Press dampened
moss into the base, and wind the
tape around it to hold it in place;
make a wire hook at the top. Poke
in the cuttings thickly all around.

☐ *Check when completed*

❧ TIP 286 ❧

Make evergreen swags for your
holiday décor. (Magnolia leaves are
great for this!) Use cuttings
from your yard or the woods; strip
their bases up a few inches.
Twist florist's wire around the ends,
and then attach them along the
length of wire or rope. Using
enough greens will hide the
wire from view.

☐ *Check when completed*

❧ TIP 287 ❧

Are you leaving some office plants on their own while you take some time off? Make sure they'll survive your absence. Soak them well one last time. Then group them in a bright spot with indirect light only. Loosely drape a large, clear plastic bag (such as a dry-cleaning bag) over them like a tent.

☐ *Check when completed*

❖ TIP 288 ❖

If you travel anywhere with
live plants, protect them. Water
them a few hours before you leave.
Just before you head out, encase
them in newspaper and staple the
covering closed (florists use this
method, you may have noticed).
Warm up the car before putting
them in. At your destination, hurry
inside and unwrap them at once.

❏ *Check when completed*

❧ TIP 289 ❧

Cut Christmas trees fare best if you
recut the base before putting them
into a clean stand or bucket of
water. Various preservatives have
been suggested, including a penny, a
splash of vodka or bleach, and
aspirin. You can try these, but most
important is to remember to top
off often with fresh water.

❏ *Check when completed*

❧ TIP 290 ❧

When wrapping presents,
tuck a sprig of lavender, rosemary,
or other overwintered herb under
the ribbon. Taking the trimmings
won't do the plant any harm this
time of year. And the recipient will
be enchanted with this pretty and
fragrant reminder of summer
days in your garden.

❏ *Check when completed*

❖ TIP 291 ❖

Make some winter potpourri, to
scent the livingroom or bathroom,
to give away as gifts, or to bring
to a hostess of a holiday party. Mix
spruce or fir sprigs, berries,
rose hips, small pine or spruce
cones, seedpods, and dried flowers
and petals. Add cinnamon sticks for
fragrance. Display in small bowls.

❑ *Check when completed*

❖ TIP 292 ❖

Check potted rosemary plants, a popular gift plant this time of year. Because it is technically an evergreen shrub from the Mediterranean, it becomes unhappy in moisture-retentive or soggy soil. You might have to repot yours into a mix that has lots of sand or perlite, to improve drainage.

❏ *Check when completed*

❧ TIP 293 ❧

Live Christmas trees can
lose needles and dry out
in the warmth of your home. Even
the strings of lights generate
a small amount of heat that adds to
the stress. So keep the plant evenly
moist, and turn off the lights
overnight or when you are out.

☐ *Check when completed*

DECEMBER

⁂ TIP 294 ⁂

Both cut and live evergreen
trees dry out easily in a warm house.
For this reason, you should wait as
long as you can before buying them,
and then keep them cold, even
outdoors, until you move them
inside. Spritz them head to toe from
time to time (unless decorations
will be harmed, of course).

❑ *Check when completed*

❖ TIP 295 ❖

Make an unusual, fresh-looking,
and colorful holiday-table
centerpiece this year. Start with a
shallow tray and one or more
colorful pillar candles. Add a thin
layer of water, then fill with salad
greens, cherry tomatoes, peppers,
or other colorful vegetables.

❑ *Check when completed*

❧ TIP 296 ❧

Retrieve some of your homegrown onions or potatoes from storage, and make a hearty soup. While you're there, take a few extra moments to check that none are rotting or sprouting. If you find damaged or "iffy" produce, discard it immediately so the problem doesn't spread.

❏ *Check when completed*

❧ TIP 297 ❧

Organize your gardening
bookshelf, especially if you receive
more titles as gifts during the
holidays. Separate factual references
from reading-for-pleasure titles.
Group the references by subject, or
by season—whatever makes the
most sense to you. Then, pick one
and put it on your bedside table!

☐ *Check when completed*

❖ TIP 298 ❖

Since light is low this time of year,
some of your houseplants might be
suffering a bit. If they're developing
lanky stems or yellow leaves, or if
the entire plant is leaning towards
the nearest light source, it's time to
intervene and help. Move them,
even if temporarily, to a brighter
spot—a sunnier, south-facing
window or under lights.

❑ *Check when completed*

⚜ TIP 299 ⚜

Is there a spot you neglected to
mulch? Even if the ground
is frozen or snow has fallen, it's
not too late. Scoop on the mulch
anyway! Its natural warmth
will melt any snow and it will settle
into place over the plants or
area you want to protect.

☐ *Check when completed*

❖ TIP 300 ❖

Safety first, always! Lock
pesticides up out of the reach
of children or pets. Also,
it's important to store all
garden pesticides where they
will not freeze.

❏ *Check when completed*

❧ TIP 301 ❧

Hang a wall calendar for the coming year, one with big squares that you can write gardening notes and ideas onto. Tack it up at eye level in a high-traffic spot so you will refer to it often. (Maybe you received one with a gardening theme as a gift—if not, they go on sale about now!)

☐ *Check when completed*

❧ TIP 302 ❧

Planning a big project or installation this year, such as a new patio or terrace, a water garden, or a pergola? It's not too soon to start researching the idea and getting design ideas from books, magazines, and the Internet. And if you think you will need hired help, line up somebody right now—before his or her calendar fills.

❏ *Check when completed*

❧ TIP 303 ❧

Inventory your seed stash. Some leftovers from last year may still be good, assuming you stored the packets in a dry, cool place. Larger seeds (beans, squash, nasturtium, and morning glory) are more likely to be viable than small seeds (carrots, lettuce, columbines, and poppies). Tiny seeds are less able to retain moisture.

☐ *Check when completed*

❖ TIP 304 ❖

Know before you sow! Slightly dampen paper towels and lay them on a cookie sheet; arrange some old or questionable seeds (about an inch apart). Cover with another damp paper towel, encase the project in a plastic bag, and set in a warm place (at least 65 degrees Fahrenheit). Check back in a few days; ideally at least half should have sprouted.

❏ *Check when completed*

❖ TIP 305 ❖

Time to shop! Gather all
your current seed catalogs. Then
cruise through them with a pack of
yellow sticky notes, flagging pages
with items you want. Compare
similar varieties and look for new
items. Compare prices, check
shipping charges, and make a wish
list. Then pare down the list
to fit your budget.

☐ *Check when completed*

✤ TIP 306 ✤

Order your seeds—for
flowers, as well as vegetables—
sooner rather than later.
Mail-order seed companies get very
busy in the next month or so,
and early orders are fulfilled faster.
Plus you are more likely to get
exactly what you want, with no
substitutions or rain checks.

❑ *Check when completed*

❧ TIP 307 ❧

It's time to stock up on basic seed-starting supplies! You need shallow flats and small pots with drainage holes in the bottoms, labels, several bags of sterile soilless potting mix (available right now at home-supply stores and garden centers), and some plastic wrap for temporary coverings.

❏ *Check when completed*

✦ TIP 308 ✦

Decide where you'd like to
keep your developing seedlings, and
prepare or clear out the area.
Choose a warm area free of drafts. If
there is no or poor light, you can
provide artificial light. Fluorescent is
better than ordinary light bulbs, or
you can buy special "grow lights."

❑ *Check when completed*

❦ TIP 309 ❦

Kill winter weeds by using
a post-emergent weed killer. These
are sold in granular form at garden
centers now; check that the product
you choose attacks the weeds you
have. (When in doubt, ask someone
for help.) Apply on a warm
afternoon, and follow label
directions carefully.

❑ *Check when completed*

❖ TIP 310 ❖

"Stratify" seeds that need it, including some perennials or wildflowers. They actually won't germinate unless they get a month or two of winter cold and moisture. Supply this by sowing them into a garden bed now or into flats that you keep outside. Which seeds need stratification? The seed packet will tell you, and tell you for how long.

❏ *Check when completed*

❧ TIP 311 ❧

This may be your Year of the Rose!
Check out the All-America Rose
Selections winners; results are
announced in newspaper gardening
columns and winter issues of
gardening magazines (or you can
visit *www.aars.org*). Thumb through
a good book on the topic by an
expert, such as *A Year of Roses* by
Stephen Scanniello.

❏ *Check when completed*

❧ TIP 312 ❧

Order bare-root roses, or buy them locally. These are dormant plants and look like a bundle of twigs, but they are actually two-year-old, field-raised plants that the nursery has kept in cold storage over the winter. They often end up being healthier, huskier plants than the potted ones you see later in the season.

❏ *Check when completed*

❧ TIP 313 ❧

If you've always wanted to grow a bush fruit, now is the time to start planning. A spot in full sun is most important. The type of soil depends on the type of plant—for instance, rabbiteye blueberries like acidic soil. Read up on your options, and be sure to note expected mature size so that you allow enough space.

❑ *Check when completed*

❧ TIP 314 ❧

This is a fine time to repot your houseplants. They may be potbound, or the soil mix may be compacted or worn out. Your plants will repay you with a fresh surge of growth. Remember to accommodate special needs—African violets like a more peaty mix; succulents prefer extra sand or perlite for better drainage.

❑ *Check when completed*

❧ TIP 315 ❧

Inventory and clean your pot collection. New ones are not cheap, and it's easy to get the old ones back into shape. First, scrape out any residue. Soak very dirty pots in a tub or scrub them with a sponge. Finally, sterilize everything in a diluted bleach solution (1 part bleach to 10 parts water) and air-dry.

❏ *Check when completed*

❧ TIP 316 ❧

Amaryllis plant all done blooming?
Pinch off the fading flowers (but
not the stalk) before the plant
expends too much energy trying to
go to seed. Move the plant to a
sunny window; continue to
water it and lightly feed it. The
more and healthier leaves it has,
the more of a flower powerhouse
it will be next winter.

❑ *Check when completed*

❧ TIP 317 ❧

Make a holding or "nursery"
area in a sheltered part of your yard.
Clear it out, define its boundaries
with a low fence or some rocks, and
put in some organic matter. You can
temporarily plant ("heel in") bare-
root shrubs, trees, and rosebushes
here until they are ready to go into
their permanent home.

☐ *Check when completed*

❖ TIP 318 ❖

Review new-plant information
in the gardening magazines.
These annual roundups usually
appear in the January or February
issue of all the major publications
and are great fun to read and dream
over. Here you can learn about a
brand-new disease-resistant rose
or a good new hot pepper.

❑ *Check when completed*

❧ TIP 319 ❧

Start flower seeds indoors in flats
or pots. Some require light to
germinate and must be laid on the
surface of a flat of seed-starting mix
or sand. Others can be covered
lightly. The seed packet will have
this information. Then place them
in a warm, draft-free spot.

☐ *Check when completed*

❧ TIP 320 ❧

Start cool-weather vegetables such as broccoli and its relatives. These need time to become sturdy seedlings so they can be the first ones out into the garden when winter is over but before hot weather arrives (they do poorly in hot weather). Try to start them six to eight weeks before you plan to transplant.

❑ *Check when completed*

❖ TIP 321 ❖

Check on stored vegetables such as onions, garlic, and squash. They should be in a cool, dark place such as the basement or garage. Pull out and discard any that have sprouted, have soft spots, or are starting to rot. They won't be good to eat, plus the problem could spread.

❑ *Check when completed*

❧ TIP 322 ❧

Tune up your hand tools.
With a damp rag, wipe metal
surfaces clean of last year's encrusted
dirt, caked-on sap, or other crud (or
soak or chip it away). Use coarse
sandpaper or steel wool to sand off
rust spots. Finally, wipe all blades
clean with a rag soaked in linseed oil
(or substitute vegetable oil from
your kitchen).

❑ *Check when completed*

❧ Tip 323 ❧

Find out when the last frost is
predicted to occur in your area.
Check your local paper, or call a
garden center or nearby Cooperative
Extension office. It's usually not till
March or April, depending on where
you live. This information will help
you plan out the coming weeks.

☐ *Check when completed*

❖ TIP 324 ❖

Sharpen your cutting tools. This
means clippers and loppers, of
course, but also shovels and hoes.
Use a file to restore the original
bevel. If the tool is unwieldy, hold it
in place with a vise grip while you
work. When finished, store the tools
in a cool, dry place.

❑ *Check when completed*

❧ TIP 325 ❧

Join a plant society. For modest
dues, this is a great way to get information and meet others who share
your enthusiasm for a certain type
of plant. Benefits may also include
regular meetings, plant swaps,
plant shows with awards, and
helpful publications. To find one,
scan the classified ads of gardening
magazines or search the Internet.

☐ *Check when completed*

❦ TIP 326 ❦

Bring more pots of sprouting forced bulbs from their cold storage into the house proper. Water them well, and place them in bright but indirect light. To help the flowers last longer, don't display them anywhere close to a heat source, particularly not on a mantelpiece.

☐ *Check when completed*

JANUARY

❧ TIP 327 ❧

Note weather and garden events
on your calendar or in your
garden journal. Record animal and
bird activity, as well as early
signs of plant life. If you get into
this habit, you'll find the
information really useful in the years
to come, when you are looking
for patterns or want to get an early
start on an outdoor project.

☐ *Check when completed*

❧ TIP 328 ❧

Have the seeds you started
indoors begun to poke their heads
up? When the first true set of
leaves appears (technically the
second set; the leaves look different
from the first, lowest ones),
use a small pair of sharp scissors
to thin out smaller or weaker
seedlings right at soil level.

☐ *Check when completed*

❧ TIP 329 ❧

Inventory your garden supplies to
see whether you are running low
on anything. Garden stores are
already restocking, and though
it seems a bit premature, there's no
harm in going shopping now to
get what you anticipate needing—
pesticides, herbicides, fertilizers, soil
amendments, stakes, plant labels,
maybe even a new tool or two.

☐ *Check when completed*

❧ TIP 330 ❧

If your orchids aren't blooming,
or have inflorescences with buds
that haven't yet opened, the
wait can be excruciating. Nudge
things along by feeding the plants
once a month with orchid fertilizer
(diluted according to the label
directions). Raising the temperature
or humidity may also help,
depending on the type of orchid.

❏ *Check when completed*

❧ TIP 331 ❧

In late winter, ornamental grasses, as well as mondo grass and liriope, start to look disreputable. Use sharp clippers and chop them down to a few inches above soil level. This "haircut" not only improves their appearance, but also makes way for the fresh flush of growth to come.

☐ *Check when completed*

❖ TIP 332 ❖

Do your favorite houseplants suddenly have dry edges or brown leaves? Low humidity is the culprit, a common problem this time of year. There are several ways to bring them relief: Spritz them occasionally; place them on a tray or dish of pebbles so runoff water can evaporate around them; or place plants closer together.

❑ *Check when completed*

❧ TIP 333 ❧

Prune your rosebushes while
they are still dormant. This is the
time to take out any remaining
damaged canes, as well as crowded
and crossed stems. You may
then shorten undamaged canes in
order to shape the plant—but
never by more than one-third
at any one time.

❏ *Check when completed*

❖ TIP 334 ❖

Prevent damping-off disease, a fungus that attacks developing seedlings, causing them to shrivel and die right at soil level. The fungi thrive in stagnant air and high humidity. An ounce of prevention is worth a pound of cure, so use clean containers and a sterile, soilless seed-starting mix.

❑ *Check when completed*

❧ Tip 335 ❧

Some of your bushes and trees, as
well as your roses, may have suckers
emerging from the roots. (Rose
suckers are below the graft.) These
are easier to spot this time of year.
Cut them off cleanly at ground level
with sharp loppers so they never
have a chance to start growing and
stealing energy from the main plant.

☐ *Check when completed*

❦ TIP 336 ❦

Plant peas! The seeds can go
in around a month before your last
expected frost date. Some soil
preparation is always important,
but peas seem to have a particular
need for nitrogen. Pick up some
"legume inoculant" at the garden
center, and add it to the patch
before planting.

❑ *Check when completed*

❧ TIP 337 ❧

Carefully water flats and pots of
developing seeds. Watering from
above may be too rough—the seeds
may be so small and fragile that they
can be easily knocked over or
dislodged. Instead, set their container
in a slightly larger one of water (even
on a cookie sheet) and let them slurp
up water from the bottom.

☐ *Check when completed*

❖ TIP 338 ❖

Buy a watering wand. It attaches
to the end of a hose and
delivers a softer, soaking spray that
is ideal for watering seedlings and
new transplants without knocking
them over. Look for one that
has a handy thumb-operated on-off
valve. Some models have several
settings, so you can choose from
mist, gentle shower, or jet spray.

❏ *Check when completed*

❧ TIP 339 ❧

Head off lawn-mowing
challenges by displaying your
birdbath, sundial, garden bench, or
other décor up on paving blocks.
Seat the paver securely in the
ground. Don't forget to check that
it's level (this is particularly
important if you are using more
than one to support a single item).

❏ *Check when completed*

❧ TIP 340 ❧

It's time to undertake serious pruning of your grapevine, while it's still dormant. This not only keeps the plant healthy and helps it bear the best-tasting fruits, but keeps the harvest within reach. Cut off at least three-quarters of last season's growth, chopping all the way back to a handful of buds per cane. Sounds harsh, but it pays off!

❏ *Check when completed*

❖ TIP 341 ❖

Impatient? Force branches of
flowering shrubs into early bloom.
Cut stems with swelling buds from
forsythia, daphne, peach, flowering
quince, or cornelian cherry. Split
the base of the stems about an inch
to increase water absorption.
Arrange them in lukewarm water
and keep them in a warm room.

❏ *Check when completed*

❧ TIP 342 ❧

Order bare-root roses, or buy them
locally. These are dormant plants
and look like a bundle of twigs, but
they are actually two-year-old, field-
raised plants that the nursery has
kept in cold storage over the winter.
They often end up being healthier,
huskier plants than the potted ones
you see later in the season.

❏ *Check when completed*

❧ TIP 343 ❧

You can now plant spring-blooming
bulbs, such as tulips, crocuses, and
hyacinths, out in the yard into a
prepared bed. Be sure to buy only
the pre-cooled bulbs, or use those
bulbs for which you had provided a
winter chilling period. Otherwise,
the plants won't perform.

☐ *Check when completed*

❧ TIP 344 ❧

Start a strawberry patch in a sunny
site. Since strawberries have shallow
roots, the soil should be loose and
free of rocks and roots to a depth of
several inches. Add a couple of
inches of organic matter. When
planting, allow each plant about a
square foot of space; set the crown
just above the soil line.

❑ *Check when completed*

❧ TIP 345 ❧

Pamper a Valentine's bouquet of
roses so it will last as long as
possible. To do this, prepare a vase
of lukewarm water and stir in the
preservative powder from the
florist.
Then recut the stems on an angle
(to increase water uptake). Set the
arrangement in a cool room
overnight to plump up. Then
display in a bright room.

❏ *Check when completed*

❖ TIP 346 ❖

Wilder areas of the yard may need some attention. Congested, overcrowded conditions are not good for the health of plants as they compete for resources. Just do some judicious thinning, and toss the discards on the compost pile.

❑ *Check when completed*

❖ TIP 347 ❖

Plan to set out a rain barrel.
This is a thrifty way to collect water
for your garden. You won't be able
to move it later—too heavy—so
choose a spot where branches or
buildings won't obstruct it, it won't
be in the way, and where it will not
create an eyesore for your neighbors.
Place a screen over the top to
keep out debris, bugs, and dirt.

❑ *Check when completed*

❧ TIP 348 ❧

Rejuvenate old, overgrown
hedges this time of year. Cut back
to knee-height or lower (if
the hedge is healthy otherwise).
Always use sharp pruners
or loppers.

❑ *Check when completed*

❧ TIP 349 ❧

Check on all your developing
seedlings. Remember to water
before feeding, or at the same time,
so the roots can take up the
nutrients. If the seedlings are
leaning towards the light source,
move the pots a quarter turn each
day to encourage the stems
to grow upright.

❑ *Check when completed*

❧ TIP 350 ❧

You may now prune your fruit trees, while they are still dormant (that is, before buds show any green). Take out dead and winter-damaged wood, suckers, and branches that rub against one another. Thin the interior so it's not crowded or twiggy, and shape the tree overall.

❑ *Check when completed*

❖ Tip 351 ❖

Keep a close eye on your
fruit trees. As soon as the buds
begin to swell, you may spray them
with dormant oil. To be effective,
the temperature must be over 45
degrees Fahrenheit. This mainly
helps to control scale, but it thwarts
other pests, as well.

❏ *Check when completed*

❧ TIP 352 ❧

Repair your lawn chairs! First, remove any broken or frayed webbing. Then buy a roll of nylon webbing at the hardware store— matching it in terms of width and color. Cut it to length, weave it through the existing bands, and fold the ends to reinforce the pressure points. Then secure the ends with snug-fitting screws.

❏ *Check when completed*

❖ TIP 353 ❖

Install edging around beds and lawn areas. Take a look at the choices at the home-supply store or garden center: metal, brick, cedar shakes, plastic, concrete, and stone. Whatever you decide, it's a good idea to dig a trench. This not only defines your line and holds the edging, but should help keep encroaching plants at bay.

❏ *Check when completed*

❖ TIP 354 ❖

Here's an easy way to fulfill an ambitious plan for a splashy bed of annuals ("bedding plants"). Decide what you want, draw up a to-scale plan, and figure out how many plants you will need. Then contact a local nursery with a greenhouse and ask them to grow them just for you. Remember to specify colors.

❏ *Check when completed*

❖ TIP 355 ❖

It's easy to plant a small tree or shrub; you can do it before lunch. Dig an ample hole. Have some organic amendments on hand to mix with the native soil. Lower the plant into place, check that it is straight and oriented pleasingly, then backfill and tamp the soil down as you go. Water well.

❏ *Check when completed*

❖ TIP 356 ❖

Vegetable garden growing too slowly? Leaves looking a bit yellow? Apply a sidedressing of higher nitrogen fertilizer to give the plants a boost (be careful not to get any directly on the plants). Crops that respond really well to this treatment include broccoli, cabbage, cauliflower, chard, and lettuce.

❑ *Check when completed*

❧ TIP 357 ❧

Pick out or make up a planting area
with excellent drainage, and fill it
with bulbs of summer bloomers.
Favorites include spider lily, crinum,
calla lily, and rain lily. Do not plant
too deeply or closely. Water the bed
lightly afterwards, and maintain
even moisture over the coming
weeks to give them a good start.

☐ *Check when completed*

❧ TIP 358 ❧

A containerized rose can be planted
anytime now. Dig a hole bigger than
the pot, and have some extra organic
matter ready to add to it as you
plant. Ease the plant out, and loosen
dense roots with your fingers.
Replant at the same level it was in
the pot, and water well.

❑ *Check when completed*

FEBRUARY

❖ TIP 359 ❖

Keep watering your small transplants. Remember: Too much water and the roots will rot, but too little and they will be stressed— possibly to the point of death. Water to soak the soil, and let it dry out between waterings. Morning is the best time to water.

❑ *Check when completed*

FEBRUARY

❖ TIP 360 ❖

Expand your resource
base by adding a book to your
library. Cool Springs Press
specializes in state and regional
gardening books. Visit
www.coolspringspress.net
or check out the list in the
back of this book!

☐ *Check when completed*

❧ APPENDIX ❧

PLANT INVENTORY/HISTORY

name _____

when planted _____

where planted _____

size _____

source _____

price _____

name _____

when planted _____

where planted _____

size _____

source _____

price _____

PLANT INVENTORY/HISTORY

name _____

when planted _____

where planted _____

size _____

source _____

price _____

name _____

when planted _____

where planted _____

size _____

source _____

price _____

Plant Inventory/History

name _____

when planted _____

where planted _____

size _____

source _____

price _____

name _____

when planted _____

where planted _____

size _____

source _____

price _____

Plant Inventory/History

name _____

when planted _____

where planted _____

size _____

source _____

price _____

name _____

when planted _____

where planted _____

size _____

source _____

price _____

PLANT INVENTORY/HISTORY

name _____

when planted _____

where planted _____

size _____

source_____

price_____

name _____

when planted _____

where planted _____

size _____

source_____

price_____

Plant Inventory/History

name _____

when planted _____

where planted _____

size _____

source _____

price _____

name _____

when planted _____

where planted _____

size _____

source _____

price _____

Today In My Garden

_____

_____

_____

_____

_____

_____

_____

_____

_____

_____

_____

TODAY IN MY GARDEN

_____

_____

_____

_____

_____

_____

_____

_____

_____

_____

TODAY IN MY GARDEN

_____

_____

_____

_____

_____

_____

_____

_____

_____

_____

_____

TODAY IN MY GARDEN

My Favorite Sources

_____

_____

_____

_____

_____

_____

_____

_____

_____

_____

My Favorite Sources

_____

_____

_____

_____

_____

_____

_____

_____

_____

_____

OTHER GREAT BOOKS

FROM COOL SPRINGS PRESS!

Gardener's Guide Series in:	ISBN
Alabama & Mississippi	1-59186-118-7
The Carolinas	1-59186-049-0
Florida	1-59186-478-5
Georgia	1-59186-044-X
Louisiana	1-93060-486-6
Oklahoma	1-59186-124-1
Tennessee & Kentucky	1-59186-119-5
Texas	1-93060-439-4

And that's not all; visit **www.coolspringspress.net** to read about some of our other books!

Managing Editor: Billie Brownell
Cover and Interior Design: Bruce Gore, Gore Studios
Tip Writer: Teri Dunn
Production Design: S.E. Anderson